WEIRD FACTS ABOUT GOLF

Strange, Wacky & Hilarious Stories

Steve Drake

OVER
TIME
BOOKS

The Publisher: OverTime Books is an imprint of Éditions de la Montagne Verte

Website: www.overtimebooks.com

Library and Archives Canada Cataloguing in Publication

Drake, Stephen, 1960–
   Weird facts about golf: strange, wacky & hilarious stories / Stephen Drake.

Includes bibliographical references.
ISBN 13: 978-1-897277-25-6
ISBN 10: 1-897277-25-3

   1. Golf—Miscellanea. I. Title.

GV967.D73 2008   796.352   C2008-901330-1

Project Director: J. Alexander Poulton
Production: Alexander Luthor
Cover Image Courtesy of: Photos.com

PC: P5

Dedication

To everyone I've ever played a round with—
thanks for overlooking the odd bit of larceny, an
occasional outburst of profanity and an intermit-
tent sprinkling of unconvincing excuses for yet
another disappointing shot.

Acknowledgments

George Plimpton wrote that the smaller the ball
used in a sport, the better the book. I thank all
the dedicated historians and sports journalists
who so eloquently researched and recorded the
goofiness associated with the great game of golf.

Contents

Introduction

In 1987, a young man from the West African republic of Benin hit perhaps the most devastating golf shot in history. Mahieu Boya had cobbled together a few clubs and some old range balls and decided to go practice in an open field near an air base in Porto Novo, the country's largest city.

There were no golf courses in Benin, but Boya had dreams of seeing his name in the sports pages one day. As he swung away with an iron, Boya made good contact. The ball went slicing high over a fence surrounding the adjacent air base and slammed into a circling bird, stunning it.

Below, a French-built Mirage fighter jet was being taxied on the runway. Just as the pilot was about to close the canopy of the open cockpit in preparation for take off, the stricken bird crashed into his helmet. The impact and subsequent havoc the now-conscious bird wreaked inside the cockpit caused the pilot to lose control of the plane.

The jet veered off the runway and plowed into a parked row of four other Mirage fighters. One by one the planes exploded, and Benin's entire air force erupted into flames. Fortunately, the pilot escaped with minor injuries, but Boya was arrested, thrown in jail and charged with hooliganism.

The story was picked up around the world—great fodder for the lighter side of the news that people in the media now like to highlight to give us a break from the otherwise endless onslaught of murder and mayhem.

Meanwhile, for poor Boya, things looked bleak. His attorney said he had no chance of winning the case. The prosecutors were willing to drop all charges if he agreed to restitution. Boya was making $275 per year. It would cost $40 million to replace the fighter aircraft. At his current salary, it would have taken Boya 145,000 years to pay off his debt to society. Not surprisingly, Boya chose to stay in jail and serve a short sentence. The toughest condition upon his release from prison was that he had to promise never to play golf again.

For anyone bitten by the golfing bug, the court's ruling would be nearly as devastating as confinement. Golfers will do almost anything to play a round. They will carve out courses in conditions ranging from the permafrost of the Arctic to the sands of the Sahara. One of the driving forces behind daylight savings was a businessman named William Willet, who lobbied to have more daylight hours to pursue his passion for golf.

The many facets of golf contribute to a history of the strange and unusual. The game is played outdoors on large tracts of land, so unpredictable elements such as weather, geography and local wildlife are necessarily a part of the game. Players have been hit by lightning, fallen into quicksand and been chased by lions.

An unknown author once wrote, "Golf can best be defined as an endless series of tragedies obscured by the occasional miracle." It's the promise of those miracles, such as Otto Bucher's hole-in-one at the age of 99, that keeps us hooked. The tragedies are also memorable, especially if we're watching a professional fall apart. Sportswriters unkindly call it "choking," and many of the best players have botched shots to lose tournaments. Their stories have become part of the game's folklore because all golfers can identify with the abrupt cruelness of the game.

And then there's an even more merciless fate—the dreaded "yips," the sudden inability to make a close putt or to hit a drive onto the fairway. For players afflicted with this form of performance anxiety, a game that once promised pleasure becomes a grim test of endurance. In his 1985 book *Golfing*, Henry Beard sums it up: "Duffers who consistently shank their balls are urged to buy and study *Shanks—No Thanks* by R.K. Hoffman, or in extreme cases, M.S. Howard's excellent *Tennis for Beginners*."

Golf, more than any other sport, offers almost endless solutions to the yips and other maladies. There are gadgets and gizmos to help find the perfect swing. These devices promise miracles, but usually the golfer just ends up looking like a goof, strapped to some chunk of plastic designed to keep a rogue body part from moving the wrong way.

Fortunately, golf is not taken too seriously by even some of the best players. Lee Trevino, the "Merry Mex," has a well-earned nickname for bringing a humorous touch to each tournament. Even after getting fried by lightning, Trevino came back with a zinger of his own: "If you're caught on a golf course during a storm and are afraid of lightning, hold up a one iron. Not even God can hit a one iron."

Golf can be played by anyone. Once reserved for wealthy and privileged men, the sport now welcomes women, children, seniors, minorities and players with physical limitations. The Golf Nuts Society of America tracks the exploits of the more passionate players of the game. Members have been known to play a round of golf in the morning and then rush to a chapel in the afternoon to get married.

In 1922, the Dixmoor Golf Club near Chicago installed speakers around the course so members could listen to church services while playing their Sunday morning round. "Pastors are complaining that members of their congregations prefer playing golf to going to church," said O.C. Upham, president of the club. "Of course, we can't take the golfers to church, but we can, and will, take the church to the golfers."

Some of society's flakiest have taken up the game, with often amusing results. Billionaire Howard Hughes used to hire naked starlets to distract his opponents. Mobster Al Capone shot himself in the foot during a round of golf. Harpo Marx played 18 holes clad in only a shirt and underwear. W.C. Fields wore pajamas on the course each Sunday.

When you throw in golf hustlers, trick-shot artists and the temper tantrums of the game's best players, golf is a goldmine of weird and wacky tales. Writer Harold Segall summed up why golf provides a bountiful harvest of the abnormal: "Golf is not just an exercise; it's an adventure, a romance...a Shakespeare play in which disaster and comedy are intertwined."

Chapter One

Extreme Golf

Golf is played everywhere. In the most remote pockets of land on every continent, there is some fanatic willing to whack a few golf balls on some desolate parcel of property. Peter Dye, the famous course designer, best described the conditions that golfers would put up with to play their pastime: "The ardent golfer would play Mount Everest if somebody put a flagstick on top."

The Yellowknife Midnight Classic

Each June, on the weekend closest to the longest day of the year, hundreds of adventurous golfers descend on Canada's most northerly city to play in the Midnight Classic. The fairways and greens of Yellowknife's only golf course, set in the bog and tundra of the Far North, are never dark during the summer solstice; the daylight is interrupted only by a brief twilight.

The tournament began in 1962 as a marathon event. Starting on the Friday night, the golfers were not allowed to rest—food had to be eaten on the go, and bathroom breaks were taken between shots. Caddies worked eight-hour shifts. In 1970, a local player named Sandy Hutchinson played a record 171 holes during 35.5 hours of continuous golf. The next year, the format changed to a much saner stroke play tourney, where every three hours, golfers are sent out on the course in a shotgun start. The ceremonial first shot is always hit at the stroke of midnight.

Yellowknife is a land of extremes, set on the fringes of the wilderness. The constantly lit but brief summer gives way to a brutal winter with four hours of light each day and temperatures that dip to −65°F (−55°C). The course was hacked out of the brambles in 1948—the greens were actually sand that had been flattened down and saturated each year with gallons of heavy bunker oil to make them smooth. The first clubhouse was the fuselage of a DC-3 that had crash-landed at the nearby airport in 1949.

Apart from the course's geography, the golfers have to contend with ravens that swoop down to steal hundreds of golf balls each year. It happens so frequently that a local rule allows players to replace stolen balls without a penalty. Besides the ravens, the first golfers had to contend with black bears that liked to frolic on the oiled greens and wolves that made a game out of taking the flags off the flagsticks. Clouds of mosquitoes and black flies also had to be endured.

Nowadays, the fairways of the course are ankle-deep ribbons of sand that sometimes swallow up balls. The climate is too harsh for grass to survive. Players can carry small mats of fake turf with them to hit out of the sand fairways. The greens have since been upgraded with artificial grass.

Local players keep the course busy through the golf season, and over the years, word has spread about the uniqueness of the Midnight Classic. Visitors from all over the world now come to give the tournament a try. Between the night-less sky, the ravens, the sand and the bugs, the golfers encounter the most distinctive of sporting experiences.

A Lunar Drive

On February 6, 1971, Alan B. Shepard became the first person to golf on the moon. The myth that Shepard hit the ball miles and miles, for the longest shot in golf history, continues to this day.

In the early 1970s, the American space program was still enjoying the success of the Apollo missions to the moon. Shepard was the first American in space and the fifth to walk on the moon. In early 1971, the 47-year-old veteran astronaut was put in charge of a three-person crew to lead another manned mission to the moon in Apollo 14.

The voyage and landing of the lunar module were uneventful, and on February 6, Shepard and his crewmate Edgar Mitchell began working on the moon's surface. After completing their tasks during the first four hours of the moon-walk, the Apollo 14 commander decided to have some fun.

Shepard had taken a couple of golf balls and a club head from a six iron with the goal of hitting a few shots on the moon's surface. He had also rigged up a handle with a slot for the club head to fit into.

With a TV camera sending a grainy black-and-white signal back to Earth, he removed golf balls and the cobbled together six iron from his bulky spacesuit. The weight of the spacesuit meant Shepard could use only his right hand to swing the club. On his first swing, Shepard topped the ball; his second pushed it two or three feet in the lunar dirt. On his third swing, Shepard made contact, sending the ball off-camera to the right on low trajectory. His fourth attempt was similar to the third—a low shot that zipped sideways from the camera shot.

After the fourth shot, the audio signal that went back to Earth picked up Shepard saying, "Miles and miles and miles." A shot traveling that distance on the moon didn't seem far-fetched. With no air, there would be little resistance to any object moving above the ground. In fact, Shepard later said that the shots went between 200 and 400 yards. Mitchell claimed the balls went only about 50 feet.

Still, the fiction that Shepard had hit the longest golf shot in history persisted. When Shepard died in 1998, President Bill Clinton reinvigorated the myth of the moon shot when he said Shepard had hit the ball "miles and miles."

The Awesome Eight Golf Challenge

The player with lots of time and money can experience perhaps the ultimate golfing challenge. Within the span of one year, golfers must play eight of the most remote and climatically extreme golf courses in the world. There is only one condition: players must carry their clubs; neither caddie nor cart is allowed.

Robin Sieger, a motivational speaker and extreme athlete, and his friend Neil Laughton, who leads adventure expeditions around the globe, started the Awesome Eight Golf Challenge. Their choice of the world's coldest golf course was

North Star, Alaska. When the foxes and ravens aren't stealing golf balls, the main challenge is the cold—the record low is −66°F (−55°C)—and the permafrost, which creates an ever-changing terrain of dips, swales and mounds. Think of a Scottish links course, but a lot colder.

They decided on Alice Springs Golf Club as the world's hottest course. Set in the foothills of Australia's MacDonnell Ranges, this desert layout features temperatures that can rise to 120°F (50°C). Throw in the frequent hot winds and the menacing rocky outcrops, and you have a course on the extreme edge of the extreme.

The *Guinness Book of World Records* lists the Yak Golf Course in East Sikkim, India, as the world's highest golf layout. Set in the eastern Himalayas, the elevation of the Yak is 13,025 feet. But for the Awesome Eight Challenge, La Paz Golf Club in Bolivia was selected. At 10,650 feet, players are still advised to arrive in the area a few days early to acclimatize themselves to the low oxygen levels.

Players do benefit from the high altitude; shots fly farther and straighter. The course designer threw in a bunch of doglegs and trees to negate any advantage. The other unique feature of the course is its surroundings. La Paz is bordered by soft sandstone that, over the centuries, has been molded into deep canyons and dramatic pinnacles.

The challenge moves to the world's lowest course in Furnace Creek, California. Located in the heart of Death Valley, Furnace Creek is 214 feet below sea level. The par-70, 6236-yard layout has been ranked as one of America's toughest. The slightly greater barometric pressure results in shorter shots. Despite the flat layout, the midsummer heat will challenge the resolve of the longest hitters. By 9:00 AM, the temperature can reach 105°F (40°C), and the record high was 126°F (52°C).

The world's most southerly course is the Ushuaia Golf Club in Argentina. Close to Cape Horn, at 55°S latitude, players have to contend with the strong gusts of cold wind that blow in from Antarctica. The most northerly layout, at 71°N latitude, is at North Cape, Norway. A six-hole course was carved out of the harsh landscape, and there in the land of the midnight sun, golfers can play 24 hours a day between mid-May and the end of August.

The challenge next moves to a much kinder climate. The Ko'olau Golf Club in Kaneohe, Hawaii, was selected as the world's toughest golf course. Carts are usually mandatory, but in the spirit of the challenge, participants must walk the 18 holes. Cardiovascular endurance is required to complete the round. Nestled in a rainforest not far from Oahu's famed Pali Lookout, the course has a slope rating of 152 (113 is considered average; 155 represents maximum difficulty) from the tournament tees. Its course rating of 75.7 (the average score of the best 50 percent of rounds played by scratch golfers at the course) ranks it as one of the meanest layouts in the world. For players foregoing a buggie, that means major hill walking. The steep terrain affords beautiful views of the 2000-foot-high Ko'olau Ridge Mountains. On 11 of the 18 holes, ravines cross the fairways. The natural landscape provides such a test of golf that a local rule requires all golfers to take a one-shot penalty if their ball finds a ravine *and* to play their next shot in a designated drop area on the other side of the gully in an effort to keep things moving.

The last stop in the Awesome Eight Golf Challenge is the world's oldest and greatest course, the old course in St. Andrews, Scotland. Opened in 1400, St. Andrews is considered the Mecca of the golf world. Perhaps the most challenging hole is the par-four 17th—a 461-yard monster that features railroad sheds and deep rough as hazards.

To successfully complete the challenge, golfers must present photographic evidence and have their scorecards signed by local officials. In its five years of existence, the certificate of entry into the Awesome Eight Golf Society has been awarded to only two players.

The Longest Course

One legacy of the Tiger era has been the lengthening of golf courses to keep the top pros from shattering scoring records at tour events. The best players have taken advantage of strength training and golf technology to attack courses like never before. Almost every year, a new longest course record is set.

For many years, the lengthiest non-tour stop has been the Pines at the International in Bolton, Massachusetts. From the back tees, it measures 8325 yards—par is 73. The fifth hole is a par-six, 715-yard monster. There are two par-fives measuring over 650 yards. The course was opened in 1957, but 15 years later, famous course designer Robert Trent Jones Sr. added the extra length that has made the Pines so challenging.

Another addition to the gigantic category is the Jade Dragon Snow Mountain Golf Club in China. Playing the Tiger tees, the course totals 8548 yards, with four par-fours in excess of 500 yards each and no holes shorter than 235 yards. The challenge is less daunting than it seems at the Jade Dragon course because of its close proximity to the Himalayas. At an altitude of over

10,000 feet, shots travel nearly 20 percent farther than at sea level.

The Koolan Island Golf Club in Western Australia features a par-seven, 860-yard-long test with an extra twist. The hole is part of an airstrip at the local airport. Players must give incoming aircraft and vehicles the right-of-way.

The St. Andrews Hill Golf Club in Rayong, Thailand, hosted a tournament on the Asian Tour that featured the first par-six to be played on any major pro tour. To play the 878-yard hole, the players had a choice of fairways divided by a lake, with the green jutting out into the water. In comparison, the shortest hole in championship golf is the seventh hole at famous Pebble Beach in California—it's only 100 yards long.

The longest unofficial course is one of those off-the-wall entries in the *Guinness Book of World Records*. On September 14, 1963, a fellow named Floyd Satterlee Rood started playing the United States—coast to coast, west to east. His last shot reached the Atlantic Ocean on October 3, 1964. It took him 114,737 strokes.

Golfing with African Wildlife

Deep in the African bush, within the confines of South Africa's amazing Kruger National Park, sits a golf course that offers a unique sporting experience. The sign as you enter the Skukuza Golf Course says it all: "Beware: Dangerous Animals. Enter at Your Own Risk."

After signing the liability waiver form, golfers waiting at the first tee will wonder what the strange, deep, ominous sounds are coming from a small, weedy lake within spitting distance. Those are hippos—8000 pounds of unpredictable and sometimes aggressive animal, with incisors that can snap a man in two.

The nine-hole course plays around the aptly named Lake Panic, so the hippos are a constant presence as the round proceeds. There are no fences around the course; all the dangerous animals of Kruger Park could make an appearance at any time—lions, leopards, rhinos and cape buffalos, to name a few. The information sheet that every golfer receives before a round reads, "Do not run away! If you run, the animal will believe that it has gained the advantage, and it will be more likely to give chase." Instead, golfers are coached to look for the nearest tree to climb.

Keeping the ball on the fairway takes on a new urgency with the highly poisonous puff adders waiting in the tall grass. Even the small herds of normally shy warthogs can become a hazard if provoked. They've done some serious damage with their razor-sharp tusks to unsuspecting players.

Despite all the menacing wildlife, course officials claim that wild animals have killed no golfers during a round. However, a woman on a nearby course lost her life when she stood in the way of a hippo that wanted a clear path back to the water. Staff are often more vulnerable than tourists; they get used to the animals and let their guard down.

Each of the holes has a marker warning players about the different dangers. Lions are energetic in the early morning and late afternoon hours. In winter, buffalo and elephants are more active. The water hazards are really hazardous; besides the hippos, there are large crocodiles. Players are advised to leave any errant balls in the water.

On the last hole, a par-three over Lake Panic, players must hit above the hippo herd, which can range in number from four to over 30 depending on the season. In the early morning hours, the hippos like to graze on the course, and in spite of their bulk, they can move surprisingly fast (up to 20 miles per hour).

The course is kept in good shape despite the size of the divots taken out by elephants and buffalo. For less than $25, the Skukuza Golf Course offers an affordable and unforgettable experience.

Any African golfing experience can offer all sorts of challenges. Gary Player was swarmed by killer bees during an exhibition in South Africa in 1966. The continent was less than kind to an Aussie professional named Jack Newton. Before he became one of Australia's most successful golfers in the 1970s and early 1980s, Newton agreed to play in a tournament in South Africa. During the middle of a round, he was attacked by a swarm of voracious ants. Newton began slapping at his body in an attempt to kill the intruders. When that didn't work, he resorted to stripping his clothes off his body, including his underpants. The gallery didn't know what to make of the naked pro in front of them.

Newton was vindicated the next day when several fans were jumped by the ants. They too had to strip down, and Newton went on to win the tournament, the first of 13 victories on various tours. In 1975, he battled Tom Watson at the British Open, losing by one stroke in an 18-hole playoff. Eight years later, Newton survived a near-fatal accident when he walked into the spinning propeller of a Cessna airplane he was about to board. He lost his right arm and eye and sustained severe abdominal injuries.

After recovering, Newton went on to a successful career as a golf commentator and course designer. He taught himself how to play golf with his left hand and boasted a best score of 78.

Reclaiming Golf from the Guns

Golf, as we know it today, has been around since 1754. Over the years, there have been a lot of wars, revolutions and other conflicts in almost every corner of the world. Golf courses are large tracts of relatively open land—prime real estate for battles. But when the conflict finally ends, the course can usually be reclaimed, and the sport once again resumes its rightful place.

Keeping golf going in countries where peace has been elusive is another challenge. The Kabul Golf Club in Afghanistan was built in 1967, and except for the odd skirmish now and then, the course operated on a fairly regular schedule. That changed during the 1980s when the Soviet Union invaded the country. The army set up camp on the seventh hole, and through the occupation, the golf course was used to store tanks and artillery.

When the Soviets pulled out in the mid-1990s, the Taliban took control of the country and the course was shut down for good. Golf was perceived as a symbol of capitalism, and the local pro, Mohammad Afzal Abdul, was thrown in jail for working with foreigners. By 2002, the Taliban had been pushed out of Kabul by an American-led coalition of troops.

An aid worker named Paul McNeill worked with the now-liberated Afghan golf pro to reclaim the course. Land mines were the biggest challenge. The explosive devices had been placed all over the course. Abdul bought some sheep and let them graze on the course as a way to clear the mines. Then the property became a training ground for de-mining crews, who found the rest.

On November 24, 2004, over 40 golfers took part in the first tournament on the refurbished course. By the next year, there were 60 members willing to pay the $60 annual membership fee. The greens are still constructed of a mixture of oil and dirt, but Abdul hopes that one day, grass can be grown on the barren landscape. At least golf has returned to Kabul.

Snow Golf

Peter Gzowski, the late host of a popular Canadian radio show, led a nationwide series of golf tournaments to raise money for literacy. To get the northern part of the country involved, the first Peter Gzowski Snow Tournament was held on Frame Lake near Yellowknife in April 1990.

The Dutch claim to have invented a version of golf played on ice as early as the 13th century. Paintings from that period depict people on frozen lakes holding some kind of club or stick, hitting an object toward a target on the ice. The Yellowknife course layout was nine holes that included one elevated tee accessible by climbing steps sculpted out of snow, fairways lined by snow banks and greens made of sheer ice, protected by fringes of stippled snow.

Players quickly found out that the greens were "icy fast," and marking the ball with a penny was a problem because the penny stuck to the ice. Despite the frigid temperatures, a number of celebrities showed up to take part, and over $110,000 was raised for a good cause. The Peter Gzowski Invitational Golf Tournament for Literacy has now become an annual event.

Other parts of northern Canada host ice-golf events. The residents of Pigeon Lake, Alberta, welcome golfers to take part in an 18-hole game of Texas Scramble during mid-March. Even farther north, in Nunavut, Iqaluit's weeklong Toonik Tyme Festival in mid-April features a golf tournament held on sea ice. Some years, golfers play in temperatures around −60°F (−50°C), whacking fluorescent balls while watching for seals and polar bears.

There are a number of annual winter golfing events in some of the colder parts of the United States:

- Snow golf tournaments are part of the St. Paul Winter Carnival and the Voyageur Winter Festival in Ely, Minnesota.

- The Doc Haznow Chili Open in Crystal Lake, Illinois, has been held for over 30 years.

- There is the annual Pillar Mountain event in Kodiak, Alaska, during which players tackle one par-70 hole that plays down a mountain.

- The Bering Sea Ice Golf Classic in Nome, Alaska, is part of the Month of Iditarod Festival (featuring the famous dog-sled long-distance race). The six-hole, par-41 course is built on ice flows.

Greens in Greenland

Serious winter golfers head to Uummannaq, Greenland, to play in the Drambuie World Ice Golf (WIG) Championship. Uummannaq is located 310 miles north of the Arctic Circle. Participants must pay a $2000 fee to play in the championship and be willing to spend a week in one of the world's most northern communities. Sponsored by a Scottish liqueur company, the event is a contrived tourism promotion that started in 1999.

The only golf course on the world's biggest island is near the main airport on the southern end of the island. Uummannaq's 1400 residents, 80 percent of them Inuit, had never played the game until the world championship came to their town in 1999. Many of the 20 players who participated in the first WIG Championship were either professional golfers who were paid by the sponsors or journalists who were curious to visit one of the most isolated places left on the planet.

The visitors had a lot to get used to. Alcohol was forbidden in the main hotel's guest rooms. One year, a drunk wandered outside to lie down among the hundreds of sled dogs that are used as a main source of transportation. In the morning all that was found of him was one single button.

In the sub-zero temperatures, the plastic legs on the stand-up golf bags snap in half. The nine-hole course is laid out on the frozen waters of a fjord. The fairways are made of groomed snow and dogleg around icebergs that are 10 stories high. Stakes mark out the rough, which is actually bumpy ice. The greens are smooth ice—it's almost impossible to stop the ball once it gets going. The hole is twice the diameter of a standard golf hole. Special-optic yellow golf balls with the WIG logo are used.

One of the winter rules allows players to sweep their putting line with a broom before attempting to sink the shot. All balls in the fairway can be played off a rubber tee, and balls in the rough can be moved up to four inches to find a better placement.

A combination of the cold temperatures and bulky clothing takes about 30 percent off the distance of a standard drive. Finding golf balls that have landed in fresh snow is also a challenge. Despite the many difficulties of hosting a world championship in such a harsh environment, hundreds of spectators show up each year to cheer for the players. For Greenlanders, WIG has become a symbol that the island can build a tourism industry and attract visitors from around the world.

Chapter Two

Battling the Weather

Mother Nature can ultimately decide how a round of golf will unfold. The best players in the world easily tame the old courses selected to host the British Open each year when the wind is slack and the sky is clear. Throw in a stiff chilling breeze off the ocean and the odd shower or two, and suddenly the same pros are scrambling to survive the test of true links golf.

Lightning: The Ultimate Hazard

The United States National Weather Service estimates the odds of being struck by lightning in a single year at 700,000:1, and about 5000:1 in an 80-year lifetime. The odds are higher on a golf course. Of the 100 people killed and 500 injured by lightning each year in the United States, 20 percent of the casualties occur on golf courses. In Canada, lightning kills about seven and seriously injures 60 to 70 people every year.

Golfers are especially vulnerable to lightning strikes, and the sport has a long history of heart-break and close calls. A golf course is an open field. And a human being, particularly one holding a metal club, is a lightning rod. Throw in trees and water hazards, both of which attract lightning, and you have a recipe for disaster. Lightning strikes occur so quickly that golfers are often unaware that they are in any danger.

Fatal Disasters

In 1957, in the worst golf tragedy on record, three players were killed during an electrical storm in Scranton, Pennsylvania.

▬ ◄

In summer 2005, a 45-year-old contractor named John Needham was playing in a charity event at the Inniscrone Golf Club in Pennsylvania. It had been raining, but the weather was clearing when Needham's foursome reached the seventh hole. Needham was the passenger in a golf cart driven by his partner, John Skross. As they pulled up to a bunker, Needham stepped out of the cart to pick up his ball.

At that instant, Skross and Needham were knocked down by a blast of electricity. The single bolt of lightning was about two inches wide, with a charge strong enough to melt the gold chain around Needham's neck. Skross was unhurt, but Needham's heart had stopped. CPR failed to revive the fallen golfer, and he was later declared dead at a local hospital. The bolt of lightning that hit the golfers was the only strike recorded in Chester County that day.

The 1991 U.S. Open was held at the Hazeltine National course near Minneapolis. More than 40,000 spectators were on the heavily wooded course on the opening day when an intense rain shower hit the area.

The fans started looking for cover from the sheet-like rain and began to huddle under trees. Forked lightning lit up the darkened sky with hundreds of fans still sitting on the dampened metal bleachers. Realizing the danger, a spectator named Ray Gavin began running toward a 30-foot weeping willow near the 11th tee. A half-dozen other spectators had already taken shelter under the tree's canopy. Just as Gavin reached the tree, two quick cracks of thunder sounded, and the bystanders under the tree were all struck as a bolt deflected off the willow.

Gavin was knocked unconscious by the blast—the lightning had entered his shoulder and come out through his hip. When he awoke, paramedics were getting him ready for transport to the hospital. From his neck down, Gavin couldn't move, but fortunately the paralysis lasted only six hours.

One of the others in the group under the willow wasn't as lucky. A 28-year-old computer technician named Bill Fadell did not survive the strike. Fadell's death was the first-ever lightning fatality at a PGA Tour event. Luckily, the electrical storm never found the fans who remained seated on the metal bleachers.

PGA Pro Survivors

Several famous golfers are among the lucky survivors after being struck during tournament play. Lee Trevino and Jerry Heard were hit almost simultaneously during the 1975 Western Open in Illinois. The two were huddled under an umbrella near the edge of a lake at the 13th green during a rain delay in the second round. Lightning from a distant thunderstorm flashed sideways across the water and threw the golfers into the air.

The lightning bolt struck Trevino's bag and the charge moved up his arm, exiting out of his back. Amazingly, it was the second time the Merry Mex had been nailed by an electrical charge (the odds of getting hit twice in a lifetime are nine million to one). Heard's point of entry was his groin, where the tip of his umbrella was resting. All the muscles in his body reacted to the surge in electricity, and he couldn't unclench his hands. Two other touring pros, Tony Jacklin and Bobby Nichols, were struck by a separate bolt while waiting on the other side of the lake.

Trevino and Nichols spent two nights in the hospital. Jacklin suffered only ringing in his ears. Flooding suspended play in the tournament for a day, and amazingly, Heard came back to play the final two rounds and finish fourth. It was only a few weeks later that the full effects of the million-volt charge began to surface.

At the Canadian Open, both Trevino and Heard complained of sore backs (Nichols suffered no ill effects). They saw the same specialist; Trevino opted for surgery to repair the damage, and Heard was told that rest might do the trick.

Trevino won nine more PGA events after the mishap, but admitted that things changed after the lightning strike. "It may not seem like it, but I look at life in a different perspective," he says. "I was kind of a wild guy. It has helped me appreciate things a little more."

Heard, a then four-time PGA event winner, was bedridden for three months and sat out most of the 1976 season. Upon his return to the tour in 1977, he struggled to find a swing that didn't hurt. His back went out in Japan, his wife divorced him, he suffered weight gain and the constant pain changed him into an irritable fellow.

Before the lightning strike, Heard had one of the most consistent swings on the tour. Somehow, using a shortened swing and a bunch of good luck on the putting green, he won a tournament in Atlanta the next season. Realizing that the victory was a fluke, Heard decided it was time to see another back specialist. As it turned out, the lightning had damaged his spinal cord and cauterized nerve endings in his tissues. This time he opted for the same surgery as Trevino, which greatly relieved the pain he was enduring.

Heard struggled to find his form after the surgery. Once a cocky player who relied on his natural gifts, he was now afraid to take a full swing. By 1980, he quit the tour. Three years later, with his savings gone, he found a job as the director of golf at a Florida club, where he stayed for almost two decades.

In 1998, Heard made an unsuccessful comeback on the Seniors Tour. "When [lightning] starts to come around, I want to get out of there," he said in an interview. "We were pretty lucky to live through the thing."

Tournament officials are now much more cautious about lightning storms. Play is suspended quickly these days, even if a storm is some distance away. Some touring pros resent the interruption, but Trevino, Heard, Nichols and Jacklin approve of the extra precautions.

A Future PGA Pro Survivor

In 1987, Retief Goosen, then just a 15-year-old amateur player in Australia, was nearly killed by a strike while on a course in his native South Africa. While standing under a tree during a thunderstorm, Goosen was struck by a lightning bolt.

"Retief was lying naked and unconscious on the fairway," described his mother, Annetjie Goosen. "His clothes were burned off his body. He suffered a burst eardrum and he was rushed to the hospital, where he spent six days." He suffered no significant long-term effects except for an irregular heartbeat and some minor hearing loss. It did take several months for him to fully recover, and Goosen's mother says the lightning strike left her son a much quieter and humbler person.

Thankfully, Goosen's golf game continued to improve after the incident. He has gone on to win two U.S. Open titles and has 20 victories in other events around the world. As soon as he had recovered from his injuries, he went back to golfing at the Polokwane Golf Club, the course where he was struck down. He supports a golf academy in his hometown and claims that he never thinks about the lightning incident while playing on the links where he grew up. However, he admits to having kept the pile of scorched clothes as a souvenir of a very close call.

Defying the Odds

And then there was a fellow named Len Plato who defied the odds in a couple of big ways. While playing on the 15th hole of a course near his home in Kamloops, British Columbia, Plato was zapped by bolt of lightning. The blast threw him across the fairway and landed him in an intensive-care unit for a few days while he recovered from temporary paralysis.

Plato had survived an electrocution that left his body with enough of a charge to short out the heart monitor he was hooked up to in the hospital. The life-changing event also left him with a premonition that he would someday become a lottery jackpot winner. It took 13 years for it to happen, but on December 25, 2006, Plato won $75,000 in a special seasonal lottery.

The odds of the two unrelated happenings are eerily similar: the chances of being struck by lightning are estimated at 280,000:1; the chances of winning the grand prize in the "Christmas for Life" lottery were pegged at 333,000:1. Plato had the choice of taking either $5000 annually for 25 years or the one-time $75,000 payment. He chose the lump sum because as an avid golfer, he believed a second bolt of lightning could be just around the next fairway.

Making it Back in Time

Scottsdale, Arizona, is a popular golf destination featuring desert golf on wonderfully landscaped courses. At a Champions Tour event in Scottsdale, Simon Hobday was one of many golfers in the field who'd had his round postponed because of a rare snowfall.

Hobday left the course during the delay to rest at his hotel room, and when play resumed, he had to race back or be disqualified. Unfortunately, waiting in the bushes for Hobday's speeding car was a police officer, who pulled him over and said, "I've been waiting for someone like you all day." The nonplussed Hobday replied, "I got here as fast as I could."

⊢ ⊣

A thunderstorm passed over the 1988 Honda Classic in Florida. As the rain started, a horn blew halting play, and everyone began scrambling for cover. Joey Sindelar and his playing partners were caught on the far reaches of the course.

Luckily, as they waited next to a tee box, a van approached, and Sindelar ran out to flag it down. The startled driver didn't have much to say as the foursome piled in the van. Sindelar asked the elderly man to take them to the clubhouse.

It was only a five-minute drive across the course to the clubhouse, but in that time the rain subsided. When they got there, the tournament officials told them that play was about to start again. The players ran back to the van and asked the driver to take them back out to the course. The driver was a volunteer who was supposed to be delivering supplies to the concession stand; he didn't know the course very well and was soon lost.

"We were screaming and yelling at him," recalled Sindelar. "We're saying, 'Take us here, take us there.' He didn't know anything about the golf course. He probably thought we were car-jacking him. We got back out on the tee just in time for the whistle to start playing again."

Sindelar went on the win the tournament.

Hot Pants

The PGA Tour has had a long-established policy of not allowing their professionals to wear shorts during tournament play. It doesn't matter if it's 85°F (30°C) and 90 percent humidity; long pants are the rule on tour.

At the 1983 U.S. Open at Oakmont, the weather was sizzling, and Forrest Fezler decided it was time to protest the dress code. Before playing the 18th hole during his final round, Fezler slipped into a port-a-potty and put on a pair of shorts. Fezler had tipped off an Associated Press photographer, and the next day the wire service sent out the photos of Fezler going into the portable toilet with long pants on and coming out in shorts.

A storm rolled into Oakmont, delaying play for the final groups of the tournament until Monday. That allowed the AP photos to get on to the front of sports pages across North America.

"It was a statement. I was kind of protesting," said Fezler about his clothing switch. "I think you could wear shorts out here. You don't see anybody [in the gallery] out here that has long pants when it's 95 degrees [Fahrenheit] and it's hot and humid."

Ironically, Fezler changed his mind about decade later when he watched an Australian tournament on television. The professionals were wearing shorts, which were okay, but some of the matching attire didn't work too well. Fezler cringed when he saw Tom Watson wearing sporty knee-high beige socks. "You can see why they don't let us wear shorts," he said.

A Wet and Wild Senior PGA Championship

In May 2004, the Valhalla Golf Club in Louisville, Kentucky, was hit by nearly seven inches of rain, electrical storms, tornado warnings and flooding that turned several holes into ponds. Unfortunately, this all happened in the five days that Valhalla was hosting the Senior PGA Championship, a major tournament on the Champions Tour.

It was one of the most weather-ravaged tournaments in professional golf history. Steady rains early in the week had already made the course soggy, but that was just a warm-up for what was to come. Heavy winds hit Kentucky and neighboring Indiana on Thursday night. Some of the golfers and caddies were caught in the storm as they left the course after a practice round. They scrambled to find shelter as tornado-warning sirens went off. Many people spent a sleepless night listening to trees fall and power lines tumble around them.

After an already two-hour weather delay in the morning, play had barely begun when Floyd's Fork, a creek that flows through the course, overflowed its banks at noon because debris had dammed the normally placid channel. Play was suspended as the front nine holes turned from meadow to swimming pool. The parking lots became swamps, and tow trucks were needed to pull vehicles out.

The maintenance crew cleared the debris out of the creek, and, using pumps and a volunteer bucket brigade, managed to make the course playable in the late afternoon. By Saturday morning, only half the field had completed their second round. The earlier finishers had to wait around until dusk to start the third round. Sunday-morning rain created more delays, and it wasn't until 2:45 PM that everyone had completed the third round. Less than an hour later, tournament officials suspended play for the day because of dangerous conditions caused by a nearby electrical storm.

On Sunday night, another tornado warning hit Louisville. Many of the golfers hadn't had much sleep when they showed up for Monday's final round. As play was about to start, Floyd's

Fork overflowed again. Crews were able to dry out the course, and finally, at 1:00 PM, the fourth round began. By dinnertime, Hale Irwin had won his 40th career senior victory and declared, "I'm proud, I'm relieved, I'm hungry and I'm glad it's over."

Some of the golfers thought the tournament should have been shortened to 54 holes from the standard four-day, 72-hole format used in major tournaments. "They had the opportunity to finish 54 holes and have a winner on Sunday," said D.A. Weibring. "I know it's a major, but we're working the maintenance crew to the edge of exhaustion. And there is all this devastation in the surrounding areas."

Several people died and hundreds of homes were damaged by the week's storms. The tornado on Sunday killed a man and destroyed 50 homes in a small town 35 miles from the course.

Chapter Three

Golf as a Second Sport

Are golfers athletes? No one can deny that there's a lot of standing around in golf mixed with a bit of walking, with very little time actually spent hitting the golf ball. The pudginess of some of the pros also lends itself to criticism that the players don't treat fitness very seriously. What is undeniable is that many athletes in other sports are attracted to the game.

Golf is the second-favorite sport of a lot of professional athletes from the four major professional sports leagues in North America. Players from baseball, basketball, football and hockey have tried to join various pro golf tours after they've retired. There is a lure to golf that satisfies the need of these athletes to keep competing at a high level. And notably, some of them have enjoyed success.

Take Me Out to the Golf Course

In 1911, Connie Mack, who is still the record holder for the most victories (3731) by a major league manager, was the first baseball boss to advocate golf as a training tool. Mack realized that his players would benefit from the crossover skills of hand-eye coordination and timing. During spring training, in an effort to conserve their arm strength, Mack told his pitchers to stay away from the ball park and instead play at least 18 holes of golf a day.

Golf soon became the second sport of choice for several baseball stars. Ty Cobb, Walter Johnson and Christy Mathewson all believed that golf would help their skills in the batter's box. In 1916, the owner of the Chicago Cubs employed the reigning U.S. Open champion, Chick Evans, as a batting consultant during spring training.

By the early 1920s, golf had become so popular with baseball players that some managers believed the game was becoming a distraction to their team's on-field performance. Three teams stopped allowing their players to bring their golf clubs to spring training.

During the 1950s and '60s, several stars, including Joe DiMaggio, Mickey Mantle and Willie Mays, listed golf as their favorite hobby.

Among current major leaguers, Atlanta Braves pitcher John Smoltz is believed to be among the best golfers in baseball. Tiger Woods played with

Smoltz at Augusta National in 2006 and was surprised by his abilities and toughness on the course. Two-time U.S. Open champion Lee Janzen feels that Smoltz could play on the PGA Tour. "He's long off the tee, keeps it in play, and he knows how to manage his game. He has the mental capacity to play golf."

The Has-Beens Golf Championship

Baseball's dominant superstars in the 1920s and '30s, Ty Cobb and Babe Ruth, may have been fierce rivals on the field, but the two had an oddly enduring friendship off the diamond. Both of them liked golf. They were polar opposites in personality—Cobb the fiery competitor who scratched out hits and was hated around the league for his intense and sometimes dirty play, and Ruth the beloved home-run champion who was known for his big appetite in all aspects of life.

Tom Stanton's book *Ty and the Babe* documented the 1941 Has-Beens Golf Championship, a highly successful challenge series between the two baseball icons. Both Ruth and Cobb had made golf their main pursuit upon retiring from baseball. When details of the challenge were made public in newspapers, there was great anticipation around the country as to which legend was the better golfer.

Ruth and Cobb agreed that all the proceeds from the matches would go to charity. Actress Bette Davis donated the trophy that would be going home with the winner. In the first match in Boston, the contrasting personalities of the two greats were apparent from the first tee. Ruth played quickly; he didn't linger over shots and was a free swinger. Cobb was deliberate, taking several practice swings before each shot—he had carefully mapped out the course before the match and followed a set strategy of shot making.

Cobb won the first exhibition, beating Ruth in a match play format after 16 holes, in front of 1000 spectators who had each paid a dollar admission. Cobb shot an 81, Ruth 83. "This exhibition golf is more punishing than baseball," Cobb told reporters. "During my 24 years on the diamond, I never was under such terrific pressure as I was while coming from behind to beat the Babe. Maybe it was because both of us were so gentlemanly. He was awfully nice to me, and I tried to be equally so. Neither of us ever acted that way in a ball game."

Ruth admitted that he had expected Cobb to needle him throughout the match, much like he had on the baseball diamond.

The second exhibition was on a course in New York. Despite extensive coverage from the press, the crowd was substantially thinner than it had been in Boston. It was a tense back and forth battle; both men were tied after 18 holes. On the first extra hole, Cobb's normally reliable putter failed him, and Ruth was the winner.

Reporters who had covered both men in their baseball primes wrote that the quality of the golf wasn't important and that it mattered less who won. "The old timers in the gallery could close their eyes," wrote one reporter. "They could see the Babe in the stadium. They could see Ty out in Detroit...After all these years, it was the Babe and Ty trying to do it again. Who cares whether they can play golf? Even at their worst they were still the best."

The deciding match was played in Detroit. Cobb prepared fanatically for the showdown, taking copious notes during his practice round and spending extra time with his caddy. Over 3000 fans showed up for the match, most of them rooting for Cobb, who had played his best baseball with the Detroit Tigers.

On a boiling hot day, Cobb's calculated approach wore the Babe down. By the halfway point, Cobb was up four holes. Ruth spent the rest of the afternoon charming the gallery with his carefree banter, and Cobb clinched the series on the 16th hole. A final promotional photo that ran in newspapers across the country the next day shows them face-to-face, gently knocking fists. Both men were relaxed and beaming at each at other. Golf had brought them together again, and a country celebrated their return.

From the World Series to the Masters

The first major leaguer to make a big splash in golf was Sam Byrd, becoming the only person to play in the World Series and the Masters. He spent six seasons in the major leagues with the New York Yankees and Cincinnati Reds as a utility player. His nickname was "Babe Ruth's Legs" for his role as a late-inning replacement for Ruth in the 1930s.

He was more successful as a golfer. He played on the PGA Tour in the 1940s and won six titles. In 1945, he reached the finals of the 1945 PGA Championship (when it was a match play event), losing in a tightly fought battle to Byron Nelson. Byrd also played in five Masters (finishing third in 1941) and nine U.S. Opens.

Byrd said that the golf swing and the baseball swing were identical, but they were swung on different planes. He also credited Ruth with providing him with a tip to "stay connected" throughout the swing by placing a handkerchief underneath his lead armpit.

Trading a Bat for a Club, and Back Again

In 1971, Ken Harrelson surprised the baseball world when he walked away from the sport to become a professional golfer. It was a bold move. Harrelson was only 29 years old, at the peak of his career. In 1968, he had led the American League in RBIs.

It was a tough road for the outfielder nick-named the Hawk. Harrelson traveled with the PGA circuit trying to gain a spot by playing in the Monday qualifying events. In three years, he only made it into seven tournaments. He did qualify for the 1972 British Open at Muirfield, where he missed the cut by just a stroke. In 1981, he made the cut at the Pleasant Valley Jimmy Fund Classic in Massachusetts—he finished 75th for his best finish on the tour. Harrelson's professional golfing quest ended when he joined the broadcast booth as a baseball analyst.

In 1978, Hall of Famer Robin Yount, who played his entire 20-year career with the Milwaukee Bucks, took a two-month break from baseball to give professional golf a try. "I injured myself on my motorcycle before spring training, and I was scared to death to let anybody know," explained the all-star shortstop. Once Yount recovered, he went back to baseball, where he played for another 15 years until his retirement in 1993.

From MLB to the Senior PGA

The addition of the Seniors Tour gave several retired baseball players the opportunity to try professional golf. Johnny Bench and Mike Schmidt played in some events. New York Yankees pitcher Ralph Terry, best remembered for giving up a famous series-ending home run to Bill Mazeroski in the 1960 World Series, tenaciously clung to the dream of becoming a tour pro when he retired.

After lasting 12 seasons in the major leagues and winning 107 games, including two of his three starts in the 1962 World Series, Terry tried to qualify for the PGA Tour. Between 1974 and 1982, he appeared in five PGA events, missing the cut in each tournament. Terry then tried the Seniors Tour when he turned 50 in 1986. He played in 96 tour events and had only one top-10 finish, in the Showdown Classic in 1989 where he tied for 10th. The former pitcher had only $162,000 in career earnings but is one of few athletes from other sports to have gained full exempt status on a professional golfing tour.

The second former major league pitcher to qualify for the Champions (Seniors) Tour was Rick Rhoden. Between 1997 and 2007, he dominated the Celebrity Tour, winning 50 tournaments and over $1.5 million in prize money. In 2007, he won a Champions qualifying event to gain full exempt status in 2008.

Rhoden had a 16-year career in major league baseball as a pitcher for the Dodgers, Pirates, Yankees and Astros. He compiled an impressive 151-125 record and was known as an outstanding hitting pitcher. He once had an 11-game hitting streak, and, in 1988, he was the first pitcher to start a game as the designated hitter when he batted seventh in the lineup for the New York Yankees.

Since retiring from baseball in 1989, Rhoden has made golf a second career. He was the leading player on the Celebrity Players Tour, with the goal of becoming a regular on the Champions Tour when he turned 50. He missed out on qualifying for a regular spot on the tour for a number of years, coming close in 2003 when he missed by one stroke. In 2005, he finished in a 10th-place tie at qualifying school and earned a conditional exempt status for the 2006 season.

Rhoden has three career top-10 finishes: he tied for fifth in the 2003 Allianz Championship; tied for sixth in the 2006 3M Championship;

and he tied for eighth in the 2005 Constellation Energy Classic. He has amassed over $340,000 in career tour earnings.

In 2007, Rhoden's perseverance paid off when he tied for first at the Champion Tour's National Qualifying Tournament. During the third round, he aced the 186-yard 17th hole. His top-place finish means that Rhoden will be a regular on the tour in 2008, allowing a few more celebrities a shot at winning on their circuit.

Leaving the Past Behind

Former star slugger Mark McGwire's passion for golf has helped him cope with the growing steroid scandal in baseball. The superstar played golf in high school, but didn't play seriously again until he left baseball in 2001. In 2003, he shocked the golfing world by winning a made-for-television skills challenge against some top PGA Tour pros. He defeated a field that included Greg Norman, Nick Faldo, Padraig Harrington, Paul Azinger, Colin Montgomerie, Rich Beem, Peter Jacobsen and Dudley Hart.

It was the versatility in McGwire's game that surprised many. Not only did he win the long-drive portion with a 319-yard belt, but he also finished second in the bunker, trouble shot, putting and chipping competitions. He nailed a short-iron shot inside two feet of the pin to clinch the title.

McGwire kept working on his swing at his home course in Newport Beach, California, and in 2005 tried to qualify for the U.S. Open. The local qualifier was being held at a course near his home, and the former home-run champion was looking to grab one of six available spots to advance to the next qualifying stage.

The day began at 8:04 AM when McGwire's name was announced by a USGA volunteer. None of the 30 spectators at the tee box applauded when he was introduced. Only five people followed McGwire's group through the round, and they were there to cheer on another player.

Wearing black shorts and a logo-less white polo shirt, McGwire was just another player trying to fulfill a dream. After a birdie on the first hole, the slugger who hit 70 home runs in a single season for St. Louis in 1998 fell apart. He missed advancing to the sectionals by eight strokes.

"I really enjoy being out here and competing," said McGwire afterward. You can play all you want, but I want to continue to test my game."

As a self-titled full-time father, McGwire plans to keep his amateur status and keep playing tournament golf to improve his game. He will try to qualify for the U.S. Amateur, the U.S. Mid-Amateur (players 25 years of age and older) and state amateur events in the coming years.

"This is the most addicting thing ever," said McGwire, who has been linked to steroid use in baseball. "I have always loved this game."

The Golfing Goalie

Grant Fuhr is a Hall of Fame goaltender who won four Stanley Cups with the great Edmonton Oilers teams of the late 1980s and early '90s. Fuhr took up golf while playing junior hockey in Victoria, British Columbia, and by the time he started his pro career with the Oilers, he was hooked. Even during the exhausting grind of the NHL playoffs, the all-star goalie would sneak away on his off-days to play 36 holes on the closest course.

When Fuhr retired from hockey in 1992, he put even more time and effort into his golf game. He found it difficult to walk away from the mental and physical challenges of hockey, and golf became his competitive outlet. As his game improved, Fuhr decided he needed another challenge and began the quest for a spot on the Canadian Tour, a second-tier circuit that has become a training ground for many future PGA players.

After a couple of near misses, Fuhr was poised to earn a spot on the tour in 2004. At the spring qualifying school, he played solid golf over 72 holes, finishing 13th with a five-over score of 293. The top 15 players earned exempt status for the season.

Fuhr had started the final round in eighth place, and despite struggling throughout the afternoon, was still in position to earn a playing card until the par-three 17th hole. After just missing a long par putt, he tapped in for a bogey but mistakenly marked a three on his scorecard. After signing his name for a 76 instead of a 77 in the scoring tent after his round, Fuhr admitted his error to tour officials. The penalty for the blunder was disqualification.

Although it was the honorable thing to do, Fuhr admitted it took him a long time to get over his mistake. Instead of dreaming about another life as a professional golfer on the Canadian Tour, Fuhr has concentrated his efforts on playing on the Celebrity Tour.

In 2006, he won his first tournament on the circuit, and even though his dream of golf super-stardom will never be achieved, Fuhr says he'll keep trying to get better. "I enjoy being competi-tive, and golf brings that out of you. You have no choice. If you're not competitive, you're going to shoot a million. And you don't have to compete against anyone, you can compete against the golf course. It's fun to go out and try to shoot even-par every day."

Golf as a Third Sport?

Michael Jordan, basketball's greatest player, shocked the sporting world in 1993 when he retired to become a baseball player. His pursuit of a baseball career ended in the minor leagues, and he returned to the NBA as both a player and an owner. Once he left the hard court for good, Jordan turned much of his competitive attention to golf.

The six-time MVP liked to make things more interesting on the course by betting huge amounts of money. In his book *Michael and Me*, San Diego businessman Richard Esquinas tells about his experiences playing golf with Jordan. On the golf course, the stakes sometimes reached ridiculous heights. Esquinas claims that before his first retirement from the NBA, Jordan owed up to $1.25 million in golf-related bets.

After he retired, Jordan purchased memberships at golf courses and country clubs across the country and then would charter an airplane to the course he wanted to play. It was the only way he could maintain his privacy—he used golf as his escape from the prying eyes of a nation.

It was well known how addicted to the game he was, often squeezing in 36 holes in a day when his busy schedule allowed the time. When a reporter asked if he would give professional golf a try, Jordan answered, "I don't know if I could ever get good enough to play pro golf. I would never jump into an arena I'm not good enough for. But you know me. I'd love to do it. That's just the competitive attitude I have."

Jordan's six-foot, six-inch frame poses a big challenge. His golf swing has a huge radius, making it tougher for him to control the ball. It's the reason that you don't see too many tall men on the PGA Tour.

Davis Love III actually introduced the Chicago Bulls star to the game after meeting Jordan while he was still in college at North Carolina. He was a natural at golf, and it became his main avenue of escape from the demands of professional basketball. He lowered his handicap over the years, and the day after retiring, he scored a personal-best 69 on a course in Chicago.

In 1990, Jordan was granted an entry to play in the Western Amateur, one of the top-five amateur events in the United States. Players go through 72 holes of stroke play competition to determine the 64 who will qualify for the one-on-one match play tourney. He was paired with a rising star named Phil Mickelson, who was then the U.S. Amateur and NCAA champion. Jordan didn't fare well, failing to break 80 in either of his rounds before missing the first cut.

In 1992, Jordan played an event on the 10-stop Celebrity Tour. He wasn't very good there either, shooting two rounds in the 80s and one round in the 90s. The next season, he put up a pair of 80s and a more impressive 71 in the final round.

In 1993, he also played in the Ameritech Senior Open Pro-Am in a pairing with Arnold Palmer. On the first tee he had to face a gallery numbering in the thousands and almost missed the ball completely. His competitive nature rose to the challenge, and he was actually able to stay even with Palmer after 13 holes. Things fell apart after that, and Jordan finished the round with an 81.

"The difference between golf and basketball was that I had to learn to be as conservative as possible," explained Jordan in his biography, *The Man, His Words, His Life*. "My nature was to be more aggressive. But this game [golf] teaches you to be humble and not so aggressive. It's similar [to basketball] in how you evaluate a putt or how to play a hole to the way you evaluate how to approach a game. All of it happened in angles. The challenge in both was to figure out the angles."

The Champ

From 1937 to 1949, he was simply known as The Champ. Joe Louis was one of the greatest boxing champions in history, and during the period when he ruled the heavyweight ranks, he was one of the most admired athletes on the planet. For millions of African Americans, he was a symbol of hope and pride.

Louis was introduced to golf in 1935. From the beginning, he was passionate about the links, spending as much time practicing as training for upcoming boxing matches. His managers considered it such a distraction that they only allowed him to play golf every second day while he was training for a fight.

Louis spent hours at the driving range trying to control his powerful swing. He could drive the ball 300 yards, but he also worked hard on his short game in an effort to become a complete golfer.

As his fame grew, Louis played with celebrities such as Bob Hope, Frank Sinatra and Bing Crosby. His favorite games, however, were with friends or the top black golfers of the era. His son, Joe Louis Barrow Jr., explained how important the game was to his father: "He just loved the game. It gave him a chance to compete and spend time with his friends. He had a wonderful sense of humor, too, and he could express it on the golf course. Outside of boxing, he had no greater passion than golf."

Louis often traveled with his own pro not only to provide instruction, but also to be a partner in money games. In the cities he visited, he would scout out the welcoming municipal courses; then he and his entourage would play almost every day. Some of the best black golfers of the period were on his payroll. The combination of practice and good coaching improved the Louis' game to the point where he consistently scored in the mid-70s.

Louis was a free-spender. Even though he was the top-paid athlete in the world, he gave it away almost as quickly as he earned it. He became a major supporter of the United Golf Association, the black organization that ran tournaments across America. Louis also competed in the UGA as an amateur player. At the 1940 Eastern Open in Washington, D.C., on a public course built especially for black golfers, Louis drew a crowd of several thousand to watch him play.

The next year, he did one better. Louis put up the money to sponsor his own tournament on a public course in Detroit. Not only did the boxer provide the $1000 purse, but he also paid the entry fees and transportation costs for golfers who otherwise couldn't afford to play. In the first year, 186 of the best black golfers in the country took part. Louis also competed in his own tourney before a gallery of over 1000 people (about 25 percent were white). He shot 88-81 and quit halfway through the third round.

Louis kept working on his golf game with the goal of winning the amateur division of the Negro National, the most prestigious stop on the UGA circuit. After several failed attempts, he took the title in 1951.

In 1952, he was invited to compete in the San Diego Open, a PGA event. At that time, the PGA was strictly reserved for members of the "Caucasian race." When the invitation was retracted, Louis became incensed and decided to confront the tournament committee. The PGA held an emergency meeting and, to avoid a crisis, decided to allow Louis to play as an exempt amateur. Louis was still upset that Bill Spiller, an African American pro who had qualified for the San Diego event, was not invited to play. "I want the people to know what the PGA is. We've got another Hitler to get by."

Thanks to his intervention, four black professionals who qualified for the next tour event in Phoenix were allowed to compete. A week later in Tucson, Louis was part of the field and started out with two solid rounds, shooting 69-72. His third round of 78 took him out of contention, but the boxer had made his mark by becoming one of the first African Americans to make the cut in a PGA tournament.

Joe Louis had opened the door for black professionals to play on the PGA Tour. By 1961, African Americans were allowed access to all PGA events. It was a long and tough battle. Even after black golfers were permitted to play on the circuit, they were still denied entry into the locker room.

Joe Louis died in 1981. He had money problems after retiring from boxing and ended up with a job as a greeter at a Las Vegas casino. He also declined physically and was in a wheelchair before his death. But he kept playing golf after his retirement from the fight game. Some of his happiest moments were when he was swinging a golf club with his son.

From the Court to the Links

Ellsworth Vines was the first notable tennis star to give professional golf a try. In the 1930s, he won two tennis U.S. Opens and one Wimbledon singles title. After World War II, he switched to golf and found some success on the PGA circuit. In 1947, he finished 12th on the money list. He played in four golf U.S. Opens and three Masters. His best finishes in the majors were a tie for 14th in the 1948 and 1949 Opens and 24th in the 1947 Masters.

Frank Conner was not as successful as Vines on the court, but he enjoyed a long and profitable career on the PGA circuit. At the age of 17, he won the U.S. Junior singles title in tennis; then he became an All-American in that sport at Trinity University before playing in two U.S. Championships as a pro in 1966 and 1967.

In 1975, he became a regular on the PGA Tour. His stint as a tour pro lasted 18 years. He won just under $750,000, had a victory in the 1988 Deposit Guaranty Classic and 18 other top-10 finishes. Conner had more success on the Seniors Tour, making $2.5 million between 1995 and 2002.

Born Equal, Born to Play

Althea Gibson was the first African American woman to play professional tennis and then golf on the LPGA Tour. Born to sharecroppers in 1927, Gibson called herself a "born athlete." She supported herself by working odd jobs before meeting boxer Sugar Ray Robinson, who, along with others, supported her early tennis career. She went on to win 56 tournaments, including Wimbledon in 1957 and 1958. She overcame bigotry and won a court decision for the right to play at the U.S. Open at Forest Hills in 1950.

The lure of better financial rewards enticed Gibson to switch to professional golf, and she joined the LPGA circuit in 1963. Without experience or training, she was able to drive the ball farther than most pros, but her raw power wasn't enough to guarantee success. Her status as a world-class athlete drew spectators, but she never won a tour event in 171 attempts. Still, Gibson had the courage to stick with golf. She had an athletic grace and approachable personality that made her a popular player with fans and her fellow pros. She walked down fairways with a slight lean like she was fighting a stiff breeze. Before each shot, her brow furrowed in concentration and worry.

During the height of racial unrest in the1960s and fearing trouble, the LPGA asked Gibson to skip two tour stops in the Deep South in 1963. Gibson agreed, but the following year she played in the events and stayed in the homes of both tournament chairmen without incident.

Gibson retired from professional golf in 1977 and was named New Jersey's Commissioner of Athletics. She suffered from serious health problems later in life, including a stroke, and died in 2003 at the age of 76.

Starting Over

Currently, both golf and tennis fans are wondering if Scott Draper can carve out a professional golf career. The Scott Draper story has all the elements required for a Hollywood tearjerker.

The Australian has just released an autobiography called *Too Good*, which chronicles his amazing run of ups and downs. Draper was an Aussie tennis sensation who won the junior doubles championship at Wimbledon at the age of 18. What the public and few others knew was that Draper was battling obsessive-compulsive disorder, an anxiety illness often triggered by stress.

The illness manifested itself in the form of a fixation on multiples of three and a terrible fear of vomiting. He managed to hide it, but Draper loathed his life. Rituals controlled his existence. For nine months he was at the mercy of his OCD. In February 1993, he reached a crossroad. He had passed his drivers test and faced a grueling 10-hour drive to a satellite tennis tournament. He had never attempted a long solo journey, but to survive on the pro tour, he would have to surmount many such obstacles.

His solution was simple—he willed his illness away. "It got to the point where the stress in my life overcame the fear of vomiting," explained Draper in an interview with ESPN. "I had to stop it, and I did."

In early 1998, Draper married Kellie Greig. He knew she suffered from cystic fibrosis before they exchanged rings. He knew she would need physical therapy, massages and frequent trips to the hospital. Yet, as Draper met those off-court obligations, his tennis game thrived.

With hardly any sleep or food after Kellie had a rough night, he won his first French Open match in straight sets and made it to the fourth round. At his next tournament, he beat six grass-court players, including two-time Grand Slam champion Patrick Rafter, to win his first and only ATP championship. Draper was ranked as high as 42nd in singles.

In July 1999, his wife died and Draper fell into depression. He started drinking and gained 18 pounds. Then he took a golf lesson. It was the escape he needed to get on with his life. He went back to tennis, but golf had made things bearable again.

In late 2004, he won his club championship at Keperra Country Golf Club. By December, he earned his playing card on the Australian Tour. A month later, his two sports collided when he decided to play in the Australian Open mixed doubles event while making his professional golfing debut at the Victorian Open—both started on the same Friday.

He ended up missing the cut on the golf course, but he and his partner Samantha Stosur won the mixed doubles title—it was his first Grand Slam championship. Six months later, Draper put down the racquet for good; golf had become his passion.

Draper's obsessive personality is suited to the links. His swing mechanics are eerily consistent—he almost never mis-hits a shot. But his late start to the sport has meant he's had a lot of catching up to do.

In March 2007, all his hard work paid off. At an Australian Tour event in Sydney, Draper overcame a four-shot deficit and shot a seven-under 65 to win the title by a single stroke. "It was a bit surreal to be part of the presentation ceremony holding a golf trophy, when tennis has been my entire life," Draper says. "It's a fantastic feeling to know I'm on the right track."

Draper has remarried, and the couple has a young child. He aims to move his family to the United States, where he'll try to earn a spot on the Nationwide Tour and, if successful, give the PGA circuit a try.

Another Sport for Another Babe

Mildred "Babe" Didrikson Zaharias may have been the greatest athlete to ever play professional golf, male or female. Her list of achievements in a wide range of sports will never be equaled. In 1950, the Associated Press voted her the greatest woman athlete of the first half of the 20th century, and in 1999, ESPN rated her 10th on the list of greatest athletes of the century, the highest ranking for any woman.

Consider her athletic resume. She was an All-American in basketball, toured the country as a baseball star and won three medals in track and field at the 1932 Olympics. She was restricted to only three events by the rules at the time, but still won the 80-meter hurdles in world record time (11.7 seconds), took gold in the javelin throw (143 ft 4 in) and was awarded silver in the high jump (even though she jumped the same height as the first-place winner, judges awarded gold to the other athlete because Didrikson Zaharias had a unique jumping style where her head preceded her body).

In the 1932 Amateur Athletic Union Championships, which served as the Olympic trials, she had a legendary meet. She competed in eight events and won six of them. She earned 30 points by herself, eight points ahead of the second-place, 22-member University of Illinois team.

Well-known sportswriter Grantland Rice told her to give golf a try. While playing professional basketball and appearing on the vaudeville stage, she worked on her golf game. Within two years, Babe won the Texas State Amateur title. The USGA wanted her declared a professional because she had earned money in other sports, but Didrikson Zaharias was able to keep her amateur status. In 1946–47, she won 17 amateur tournaments back to back, including the U.S. Amateur, and became the first American to win the British Ladies Amateur.

Didrikson Zaharias then turned pro, earning over $100,000 playing in exhibitions and promotional events. As a founding member of the LPGA, Babe was the star who attracted fans to the fledging circuit. She was not only good—she won 41 professional tournaments, 10 of them majors—but she was also an entertainer.

One sportswriter said that Babe had a constant sense of theater. To warm up a gallery, she'd put on dazzling displays of trick shots. Setting up five balls on tees, she would drive them in rapid succession, getting the fifth one launched before the first one had landed. A right-handed player, she could switch to the left side and still unleash monster drives. On the green, she could make the ball hop over her foot and still find the cup. She would also toss clubs down and hit the ball with her putter so that it jumped over them in succession.

She had a stash of one-liners ever at the ready: after a long drive that sailed out of bounds, "I hit it straight, but it went crooked"; after missing a short putt, "I feel like nuts and bolts rattling together"; and to move a gallery out of her way, "I know I'm good, but not this good. I have to have room to hit the ball." At LPGA clinic galleries she would call out, "Stand back, caddie! This ain't no kid hittin." Or she would say, "Watch close boys, cause you're watching the best." In 1951 at the Western Women's Open in Philadelphia, Babe shocked several thousand spectators by removing her white nylon slip and nonchalantly tossing it to her caddy with the comment, "Too hot."

Her husband, the famous wrestler George Zaharias, was part of the act. His bad knees and big frame (he weighed over 300 pounds) prevented him from walking the course, so he drove his car around instead. When she sank a putt, George would beep his horn in approval.

Didrikson Zaharias was an intimidating presence to her competitors. She would enter the locker room and say, "Hi girls! Ya gonna stick around and see who'll finish second this week?" Once, she called several of the top players together to tell them that they were the spear-carriers and she was the star, and that no one paid to see spear-toters.

A press release from Wilson Sports, one of the tour's biggest sponsors at the time, backed up her sentiments: "Mrs. Zaharias is the player they pay to see. And as long as the galleries trail her around the fairways, the walloping Babe from the Lone Star State will get the big money."

Through the mid and late 1940s, Didrikson Zaharias dominated the LPGA Tour. She was voted Associated Press Woman Athlete of the year six times—five of those were for her success on the tour.

In 1953, she was diagnosed with cancer and had a colostomy. Fourteen weeks later, she returned to competitive golf and won seven more tournaments. In 1955, the cancer returned, and the press coverage of her decline was extensive and sensational. She died in September 1956 at the age of 45.

Chapter Four

Celebrity Golfers

No other sport in North America is as closely tied with the rich and famous. The biggest names in show business, popular music, the business world and other sports have all been linked to the game of golf. There's even a successful tour dedicated to celebrity golfers that draws good-sized crowds to its 10-plus stops each season.

The Club of the Stars

The coolest golf course in the world sits high above Sunset Boulevard. The Bel-Air Country Club is the golfing home of Hollywood. Over the years, its members have racked up a lot of celebrity points, including Jimmy Stewart, Katharine Hepburn, Howard Hughes, Gary Cooper, Clark Gable, Carole Lombard, Andy Williams, George C. Scott, Richard Crenna, Glenn Ford, Edgar Bergen, Spencer Tracy, Jerry West, James Garner, Dick Rowan, Dean Martin and Joe Pesci.

On a Friday night, Hoagy Carmichael played piano in the bar, and Bing Crosby often dropped in to try out a new song. Elizabeth Taylor married Nicky Hilton at the Bel-Air Country Club. Glen Campbell is a member; so is Bob Newhart. Johnny Carson joined to play tennis at the club, as did Mary Tyler Moore, George Kennedy and Pat Boone.

Dean Martin was the resident hustler. He would make bets in the thousands and almost always clean up. Martin was the ultimate cool dude—perfect slacks, a buttoned knit shirt and two-tone black-and-white golf shoes, with a cigarette dangling from his mouth as if it was an extension of his body.

Bel-Air may be a symbol of old L.A. money, but celebrities continue to play the course. Matt Damon, Jack Nicholson and Joe Namath are frequent guests. At Bel-Air, nobody asks for an autograph; nobody is a star because almost everyone who plays is either famous or has an extraordinary amount of money—or both.

Much of the folklore surrounding the course is Hollywood related. Robert Redford would sneak on the course at the fourth hole and play when he was kid. Also on the fourth, a scene from a Tarzan movie was shot at a hidden cave, with Johnny Weissmuller as the original King of the Apes. Fred MacMurray once aced the fifth hole, a par-three, by bouncing his ball off a portable toilet. Elvis Presley used to have a house on the sixth hole.

Howard Hughes once landed his plane on the eighth fairway because he was late for a date with Katharine Hepburn (she would shoot in the mid-80s playing from the men's tees). When the Bel-Air executive complained, Hughes vowed never to play the course again. He was true to his word, though he kept paying his membership fees.

The 12th green is called the Mae West because it used to have two huge humps guarding it. More famous people have aced the 13th hole than any hole in history: Clark Cable, Fred Astaire, Ray Bolger, Mike Douglas, Lloyd Nolan, Howard Keel and Lawrence Welk. Alfred Hitchcock used to live in a house beside the 15th hole. Red Skelton used to come out of his house near the 16th green to chat with the members. And Bobby Jones, W.C. Fields and Groucho Marx made a series of golf films on the 17th hole.

Bob Hope

No other celebrity has promoted or loved the game more than Bob Hope. The Bob Hope Chrysler Classic in Palm Springs has been a fixture on the PGA Tour since 1965. The unique five-day,

90-hole event played over five golf courses draws the tour's largest field, with 136 pros and three times as many amateurs, including the deepest field of celebrity golfers.

Bob Hope was born in 1903 and had a passion for sports as a youth. He boxed professionally under the name of Packy East and was a pool shark. He played his first game of golf in Winnipeg, Manitoba, in 1930 while performing on the vaudeville circuit. The jugglers in the act would golf to kill time between shows and invited Hope to play with them. He was soon hooked on the sport. As his fame grew and he began traveling around the world, golf became his main passion. "Golf is my profession," he once said. "Entertainment is just a sideline. I tell jokes to pay my green fees."

Hope estimated he played on some 2000 courses worldwide and took lessons from the local pro at most of them. Ben Hogan helped him improve his game (he brought Hope's handicap down to four). Hope played in the 1951 British Amateur, but lost in the first round of the match play tournament. "I got beat in the first round by a man smoking a pipe, which of course delighted Bing Crosby," he once recalled.

In 1985, he wrote a bestseller called *Confessions of a Hooker: My Lifelong Love Affair with Golf.* A compilation of his favorite anecdotes about the game, it stayed on the New York bestsellers list for 53 weeks. Golf was always a fertile ground for Hope to harvest laughs. Among the 85,000 pages of his jokes stored in the Library of Congress archives are several volumes on the sport.

It's wonderful how you can start out with three strangers in the morning, play 18 holes, and by the time the day is over, you have three solid enemies.

Hope played golf with almost every American president that came to office over his 100-year lifetime. He loved to tease President Gerald Ford about the number of spectators that he plunked in the many pro-am golf events he took part in after leaving office in 1977.

Ford is easy to spot on the golf course. He drives the cart with the red cross painted on its top.

As a supporter of the American military, he would walk on stage at shows for soldiers and sailors with a golf club in his hand—a prop he used like a vaudeville song-and-dance man might use a cane.

Besides the seven holes-in-one he nailed in his 70 years on the golf course, Hope's greatest achievement in the sport was establishing the Bob Hope Chrysler Classic. By the time he died in 2003, his golf tournament had raised over $35 million for various charities. Each year, fans, friends and family gather to remember the icon at the start of the tournament that still bears his name.

Bing Crosby

Like Bob Hope, Bing Crosby was instrumental in cultivating the game of golf in the United States. In 1937, he established the first pro-am tournament at the Rancho Santa Fe Golf Club near San Diego. Sam Snead won the $500 first place prize (and demanded his winnings in cash). Clark Gable, Fred Astaire and Randolph Scott were among the first celebrities to play in the tourney.

After World War II, the Bing Crosby National Pro-Amateur resumed on golf courses in Pebble Beach, where it has remained ever since. The February tournament became known as the Crosby Clambake, honoring the host's tradition of throwing a barbeque during the week.

Crosby invented his own vocabulary around the tournament. If you landed in a bunker, you were "in the loge." Swinging a golf club was "basting a turkey." The winter weather at Pebble Beach was always unpredictable—the annual cloudbursts were "ring-tailed twisters," requiring the fans to break out their "mukluks" (boots) and "balbriggans" (long johns).

Crosby played golf as kid in his hometown of Spokane, Washington, and caddied. Like Bob Hope, he took up the game seriously when he was involved in vaudeville during the mid-1920s. The year before he started the pro-am, Crosby won the first of five club championships at a course in North Hollywood. In around 1930, Hope and Crosby met for the first time in New York and began hitting golf balls together at a local driving range between shows.

Their friendship lasted for the next 45 years, and together they made the successful Hope-and-Crosby "Road" movies that made millions.

"Bing was always a little better than I—a two handicapper. At my best, I was a four. But mostly I was a six," recalled Hope. "Bing took the game seriously. I liked to play for laughs, but he worked hard on his swing."

Like his friend, Crosby played in the British Amateur at the famous St. Andrews course in 1950. The locals came out in large numbers to watch the celebrity embarrass himself in the match play tournament. Crosby's opponent was a Scot named Wilson. The American crooner opened with a birdie, then a par, then birdied two more holes. But nerves and inexperience caught up with him as the match progressed, and Wilson came back to win.

Crosby qualified to play in the U.S. Amateur but said his greatest thrill in the sport was watching his son Nathaniel become a top prospect. Four years after Crosby died in 1977, Nathaniel won the 1981 U.S. Amateur.

"When I was playing junior golf," said Nathaniel, "Dad would follow me for a couple of holes, just to let me know he was there. Then he'd disappear, so as not to upstage me. He'd sneak from tree to tree, thinking I couldn't see him. Or he'd watch from two or three fairways over, through binoculars. He'd have on a Sherlock Holmes hat and sunglasses. Nobody knew who the heck he was."

Using his influence with the PGA, Crosby tried to coax the tour into including a few women professionals. His persistence didn't work, but it didn't stop him from having Babe Didrikson Zaharias compete in the 1939 Crosby Clambake as a pro, partnered with her famous wrestler husband George Zaharias. Nancy Lopez later played in the tourney as an amateur in 1977.

On October 14, 1977, Crosby was happy as he walked off a golf course near Madrid. He had shot an 85 and won a $10 bet. He said, "That was a great game of golf, fellas," and collapsed a few minutes later. At the age of 74, he had suffered a massive heart attack and died.

The Crosby Clambake became the AT&T National Pro-Am. The Crosby name has quietly faded over the ensuing years, but Clint Eastwood and Bill Murray, among other celebrities, have tried to preserve the atmosphere that Bing Crosby brought to the tournament.

Dinah Shore

If Hope was the most famous patron of the PGA Tour, Dinah Shore was the number one supporter of women's golf. The same infectious charm, unassuming manner and cheerful optimism that attracted audiences to her variety show for seven seasons made the Dinah Shore Classic Golf Tournament the most recognized event on the LPGA circuit.

Shore was first asked to host the Palm Springs tourney in 1972, and even though tennis was her number one sport, the popular singer with over 75 hit songs such as "I'll Walk Alone" (1944) and "Buttons and Bows" (1948) brought the same enthusiasm to the endeavor as Hope and Crosby did on the men's side.

In 1972, Colgate signed on as the main sponsor of the Dinah Shore Tournament, attracting much-needed attention and dollars to the women's tour. The pro-am event quickly became one of the four women's majors and drew some big-name celebrities to play in it. As the March tournament grew in stature, it attracted more women and gained a lesbian connotation.

In 1990, the tourist industry in Palm Springs realized they had something bigger than a golf tournament to promote. Dinah Shore Weekend was soon billed as the "largest women's event in the world." Each year it attracts 20,000 lesbians to the resort community. The party usually includes naked frolicking in pools, comedy events and cocktail hours. The entertainment lineup over the years has included such acts as the Pussycat Dolls, Joan Jett and the Blackhearts, En Vogue and Margaret Cho.

There's even a golf tournament for lesbians called the Lina Shore Golf Classic. Founded by real estate agent Caroline "Lina" Haines in 1988, the parallel event has grown each year since it began. Over 200 beginner, intermediate and advanced players play in the one-day tourney. Local charities benefit from the dinner-dance and auction that are held the same evening.

Up to 1990, the Dinah Shore Weekend consisted of "underground" gatherings at someone's home. A younger generation of lesbian promoters then began packaging the weekend, booking entire resorts and convention space.

In 1997, *Sports Illustrated* devoted four pages to the lesbian social activities and only three pages to the actual LPGA event. The next year, Titleist, a golf equipment manufacturer, pulled a large chunk of advertising money from the magazine.

There has been some discomfort with the LPGA tournament being overshadowed by events surrounding it. Before her death in 1994, Dinah Shore insisted she was not a lesbian. Kraft Nabisco became the sponsor of the event in 1982 and removed her name from the championship in 2000. After Shore died, there were rumors that Nabisco would pull out of the tournament because it had come to be thought of as a lesbian event. The company responded by renewing its commitment to the tournament and raising the prize money. The Kraft Nabisco Championship, as it is now called, is still one of the biggest events on the LPGA Tour.

Even though her name is no longer on the tournament banner, her legacy lives on. The golf course in Rancho Mirage was renamed the Dinah Shore Tournament Course, an LPGA scholarship fund has been established in her name, and an entertainment extravaganza is held in her honor every year during the week of the event.

Bill Murray

The Hollywood actor and original cast member of *Saturday Night Live* will be forever linked to golf through the movie *Caddyshack*, which is widely recognized as the best film ever made about the sport. In the 1980 cult classic, Murray played the deranged groundskeeper Carl, a perfect role for the eccentric comedian. Over the years, Murray has become the most popular celebrity to play at the AT&T Pebble Beach National Pro-Am, the tournament hosted by Bing Crosby until his death in 1977.

The Pebble Beach Pro-Am is supposed to be about the enjoyment of golf. For four rounds, the pros play with the celebrity amateurs—it has all the tension of a regular tour event, but the gallery also has the opportunity to watch their favorite stars experience the atmosphere of the PGA as they compete in partnership with a professional golfer.

Crosby's death and the phenomenal growth in money associated with the tour has taken some of the informality out of the Pro-Am. Clint Eastwood, Kevin Costner (the star of another famous golf flick called *Tin Cup*) and Murray have been the celebrity figureheads of the tourney since Crosby passed away. Murray's zaniness—he works the crowd shamelessly, wears outrageous clothes (bib overalls one year) and has added the corniest of gag jokes (exploding golf balls)—has drawn criticism from the upper levels of golf's hierarchy.

In 1993, Murray was almost banned from the event after an infamous bunker incident. At one point during the tournament, he suddenly grabbed an elderly woman from the gallery and began dancing with her. The impromptu waltz lost its charm when the woman fell into a bunker. Fortunately she was not seriously hurt, but it took her two days of bed rest to recover.

"The Bill Murray thing was inappropriate and detrimental and will not be tolerated in the future," Deane Beman, the commissioner of the PGA Tour, declared publicly.

At the time, Murray was the event's biggest draw, and in the true spirit of *Caddyshack*, in which the stuffy, country club atmosphere is constantly mocked, the comedian fired back at Beman, calling him a Nazi. The popularity of Murray with the fans won out, and the commissioner was forced to retreat. It was probably a wise decision—even the woman who took the spill into the bunker faithfully follows Murray every time he plays Pebble Beach.

Several golf pros were also critical of Murray's actions, but over the years his antics have been accepted as part of the Pro-Am. "I thought Bill Murray went overboard, spinning the woman into the bunker," said Tom Watson in an interview. "But whether you agree with his antics or not, he has brought a lot of people out here."

"One Bill Murray is good for the tour; two would be a disaster," said Johnny Miller several years ago when asked about the comedian.

Murray's popularity can be understood in his role as a link between the ordinary hack golfer and the country club elite. He may dress like a slob, but he knows how to play. He grew up in a golf family and worked as a caddie and maintenance guy as a kid. He is known both for his wildness off the tee and for his marvelous recovery shots.

Scott Simpson, a touring pro, asked to play with Murray after several professional partners found his act distracting. Simpson believes that the comedian brings fun to the event without disrespecting the game. "Bill had the reputation of being hard to play with, and I wanted to show that you can play golf and have fun. Bill does respect the game. He keeps quiet when we putt—most of the time. He loves golf and its traditions, but he also loves to have fun out there. He's an entertainer; the crowd loves him. Everything he does is clean humor."

Alice Cooper

Alice Cooper credits golf for helping him stay alive. In his memoir, *Alice Cooper, Golf Monster: A Rock and Golf Addict,* Cooper writes about how he traded booze for birdies. The American rock singer inspired the term "shock rock" with his stage shows that featured guillotines, electric chairs, fake blood and boa constrictors.

Through the late 1970s and early '80s, Cooper went through rehab to battle alcoholism. He substituted one addiction for another when he was introduced to golf in Winnipeg, Manitoba. He's often on the course six days a week and has become a five-handicap golfer, even appearing in TV commercials for Callaway Golf.

"Every guy I know from Lou Reed to Bob Dylan to Neil Young, they all play golf," explained Cooper in an interview promoting his book. "It's because they were all drug users or alcoholics, and I think golf is so addictive that it's just like taking drugs. You know, it's like you're always looking for that next great hit. It's the same thing in golf, you're always looking for the next great shot."

Willie Nelson

One of the founders of the Outlaw Movement in country music, Willie Nelson has two passions: music and golf. In a career spanning 250 albums and over 2500 songs, he found time to buy his own golf course—not just once, but three times.

Nelson's home course is in Spicewood, Texas — a nine-hole layout called Pedernales Cut-N-Putt. "I first saw Pedernales playing in a celebrity tournament in the mid-seventies," explained Nelson in an interview with a web-based golfing magazine. "A year or two later, another guy and I bought the club. Then I let him have it, but later I bought it back. Then I lost it to the IRS, so two friends bought it back for me. The Feds said my guys didn't pay enough for it, so the IRS took it back and sold it to an Iranian fellow. We didn't get along, so I convinced a theater owner to buy it for me, and I did six months of shows to pay him back. So I guess I've paid for this course a few times."

Pedernales has become a second home for Nelson. He added a state-of-the-art recording studio to the clubhouse and incorporated a number of unique rules for the course. For example, rule number five states, "No more than twelve in your foursome." Rule number eight optimistically declares, "Please leave the course in the condition you'd like it to be found."

Nelson plays fast, zipping around the course in a golf cart with 12 or 15 friends. Everyone scatters around the hilly layout trying to avoid the many rocks and roots that litter the course.

The local golf pro is Larry Trader. Often he'll team up with Nelson to take on whoever is willing. During the 1990s, Lee Trevino visited the course every year on a side trip from Austin, where he was playing in a Seniors Tour event. "Our finest day was when Willie and I scrambled against Trevino," said Trader. "Lee shot a six-under 30 on his own ball, and we had to shoot a 29 to beat him." They did.

Nelson's intimate knowledge of the course was the source of a favorite practical joke. He would take a guest out in his cart to the third hole and drive at full speed toward a low-hanging tree limb that looked the right height to decapitate the golf cart and the people in it. Nelson knew that the branch was an eighth of an inch higher than the cart, but he never tired of watching the look on the unfortunate person's face as he roared toward the tree.

Kris Kristofferson, Neil Young and Dennis Hopper have all visited Pedernales. Whether it's the charm of the course or their special host, all of them ended up becoming golfing enthusiasts. Nelson's simple approach to the game seems to charm them all.

"People want to know everything about the golf swing," explained Nelson. "But Trader always told me, 'Just hit the ball.' It's not anything special. Little kids usually hit it great the first swing. Lots of people do. But when they start getting instruction, they go all to hell."

A President's Game

American presidents have been hooked on golf almost as long as the first courses were built in the country. In 1958, Dwight Eisenhower gave his name to the Eisenhower Trophy, formerly the World Amateur Team Championship. Ten years later, Eisenhower became the first ex-president to have a hole-in-one. In 1977, Gerald Ford became the second.

The most dramatic round of golf involving an American president took place one weekend in 1983 when Ronald Reagan accepted an invitation to play two rounds at Augusta National golf course, the home of the Masters. Reagan received some flack at a press conference for agreeing to visit the exclusive club, which at that time had no black members.

While Reagan was on the course on Saturday, a 44-year-old unemployed millwright named Charles Harris drove a pick-up truck through a side gate. Brandishing a pistol, Harris took seven hostages, including two White House aides, and demanded to talk to the president.

Reagan was several hundred yards away, playing with Secretary of State George Schultz, Treasury Secretary Donald Regan and former senator Nicholas Brady of New Jersey. When the president heard about the incident, he tried to speak to Harris by phone. On the first attempt Harris hung up, and on the second call he refused to reply to Reagan's questions.

Fortunately, Harris released the hostages one by one and was arrested two hours after the incident began. No one was hurt. Harris pleaded guilty to charges of kidnapping, false imprisonment and criminal damage to private property. He was sentenced to 10 years in prison and 10 more on probation.

Reagan never did get to complete his round on Saturday. His Sunday match was also a write-off. The president had to rush back to the White House when the Marine headquarters in Beirut were bombed.

▬ ◄

In 1995 at the Bob Hope Chrysler Classic, three presidents teamed up to do some unintentional damage. George Bush, Gerald Ford and Bill Clinton made up a foursome with Scott Hoch, a professional whose golf game ended up being much steadier than that of his playing partners.

Ford set the tone for the day at the first tee when he told the large gallery to stay behind the golfers. True to form, the 81-year-old former president hooked his drive into the crowd. Clinton was next. The nervous president sliced his tee-shot into a bunker. Bush actually kept his drive on the fairway, but his second shot claimed the first casualty. His ball hit a tree and then hit an elderly lady in the face, breaking her glasses and cutting her across the bridge of her nose.

Bush rushed to aid the woman, who was taken away in a golf cart and later required 10 stitches to close the wound. On the 14th hole, his drive claimed another spectator. This time the man was quick enough to turn his back before impact, and the ball hit him on the back of the leg.

On the 17th hole, Ford hit a spectator, drawing blood from her left index finger, but no stitches were required. At the end of the bloodbath, Bush (who was then 70 years old) edged Clinton (who was 46) by shooting a 92. Clinton scored a 93. Ford came in with an even 100, not including a few mulligans.

Taking on Donald Trump

In 1983, director John Forsythe made a charming film called *Local Hero*. Filmed along the Scottish shoreline, it depicts a beach-dwelling resident's resistance in selling his land to a Texas oil tycoon played by Burt Lancaster. Felix Happer, the Lancaster character, wants to build a refinery that would forever change the ways of the people residing in a small village.

Twenty-four years later, the plotline is being eerily repeated in real life in the small village of Balmedie, just outside of Aberdeen along the east coast of Scotland. The tycoon is Donald Trump, and he wants to build two 18-hole golf courses, a luxury 450-bedroom hotel, 950 holiday homes, 36 golf villas and a gated community of 500 pricey properties.

In the middle of this grand plan, between one of the golf courses and the high-priced hotel, is a 23-acre plot of land containing a couple of decrepit houses and a shabby-looking mobile home. The owner's name is Mike Forbes, and he's not a golf fan.

Trump has offered him $700,000 for the land, but the 55-year-old, who shares the plot with his mother, is not interested in selling. "What's the point?" he says of Trump's offer. "Where could we find to live that is more beautiful than this place?"

It's a classic David versus Goliath story. Trump visited the site of the proposed development and criticized Forbes for the "disgusting" state of his land. "There were rusty tractors, rusty oil cans," said Trump to a reporter from the UK Press Association. "I actually asked him, 'Are you doing this on purpose to try and make it look bad, so I have to pay some more money?'"

In *Local Hero*, Felix Happer is won over by the simple beauty of the dunes and the simple life of the villagers. In the end, he decides there are more important things than money. Trump is not tempted by such romantic idealism. He has already threatened to surround Forbes with his 1400-acre development.

The brashness of Trump has helped galvanize local opposition. While in Scotland, he declared his golf courses will be the best in the world—this in the country that is the birthplace of golf, with St. Andrews and several other historic courses. Environmental groups have declared the importance of preserving the sand dunes that are home to rare birds. "We must also ask ourselves if this really is the kind of development we want in Scotland," said Shiona Baird, a Green Party member of the Scottish Parliament. "We already have some of the best golf courses in the world."

An offshore wind farm has also been planned near Aberdeen, a proposal that does not sit well with the New York billionaire. "I am not thrilled," said Trump. "I want to see the ocean; I do not want to see windmills."

The proposed $2 billion development follows a number of other Trump courses and resorts that have been built in New York, New Jersey and Los Angeles. The trademark Trump development is all about grandeur, which to many people borders on vulgarity.

In December 2007, the project was given outline-planning approval, but a week later, the Aberdeen infrastructure committee rejected Trump's application. "We are having a pistol held to our heads," said committee chairman Martin Ford, who cast the deciding vote. "I don't think we should sell our souls."

Forbes said he was "over the moon" with the result. "Hopefully, Trump has now got the message that we're not a bunch of cabbages up here. We've managed fine without him up to now, and we'll get on just as well without him."

Immediately after the announcement, Trump threatened to move the development to a site in Northern Ireland. The Scottish government then took the unusual step of reviewing Trump's application. At the time of publication, the project is before the Scottish Parliament's Economy, Energy and Tourism Committee. No decision has been reached.

Chapter Five

Hustlers, Long-ball Legends and Trick-shot Artists

Some of the most fascinating and entertaining golf is played outside the professional circuits. In the early days of the PGA Tour, the pros were competing for small purses. In 1920, the U.S. Open and PGA champions pocketed only $500, and the British Open winner took home 75£. Prize money didn't increase significantly until 1960.

Professionals were often forced to supplement their income by showing fans their amazing skills with trick-shot exhibitions and long-drive competitions. And then, lurking in the shadows were the golf hustlers, who would surface wherever there was money to be won. Often disheveled, with worn-out clubs and the worst looking swings, they would hang around long enough to take a few hundred dollars in side bets from the unsuspecting locals.

The Best Golf Hustler of All Time

Very few golf fans have heard of Titanic Thompson, and that's the way a hustler likes it—anonymity is required for success on the shadowy side of the sport. Within golfing and gambling circles, Alvin Thomas, aka Titanic Thompson, rose to prominence in the 1920s and was recognized as the best in his craft for decades.

The facts often become fantastic tales in the hustler's undocumented world. Even the story of his nickname comes with several versions. Some say his first name was earned at the pool table when observers noted he "was sinking everybody around here," and he changed his last name because he liked the sound. Others claim he bet someone he could jump over a pool table flat-footed, and when he did, the other guy said, "You sank me like the Titanic." There was another report that Thompson was one of the few male survivors of the sinking of the famous passenger ship. It was written that he avoided death by dressing like a woman and slipping into a lifeboat.

Thompson had extraordinary hand-eye coordination, and as a child he sharpened his gift with hours of practice doing things like throwing coins into a little box at the foot of his bed.

The work paid off years later when he cleaned up in bets by throwing silver dollars into a golf hole from 10 feet away. He became a marksman with a rifle and pistol, a pool hustler and a poker player who knew all the ways to cheat. Golf has always attracted the wealthy, and Thompson saw the potential to fleece a whole new crowd of unwary prey.

With a little ingenuity, he turned many of his bets into sure things. He wagered he could make a 40-foot putt on his first try—with a condition that the putt took place first thing in the morning. The night before, he would pay off a groundskeeper to lay a hose on the green running to the hole. Left overnight, the hose would force an indentation in the grass, creating a path for the ball to follow.

Once, he offered a young pro three drives on every hole, with the right to choose the best shot of the three, to his one. Halfway through the round, the pro was so weary that Thompson cleaned up on the back nine to win the bet.

Another technique he used frequently was to play two rounds against the same fellow. The first time around he would lose comfortably, pay off his wagers and get a handicap. Then, with the stakes increased significantly, he started putting pressure on the poor mark by proposing side bets on every hole. As the round unfolded, the number of bets increased. By the time they were finished, there was so much money and math on the table that his opponent would unravel, and Thompson would clean up.

Successful hustlers adapt quickly to a new opportunity. One day, Thompson was playing golf with a man who had brought a champion bird dog. Seemingly out of the blue, he bet the man that he could get his dog to bark in less than a minute. The man was a dog trainer, knew his pet and made the bet. What he didn't know was that Thompson had spotted a rabbit in a nearby ditch. With his tee shot, Thompson hit a low drive that just missed the rabbit, sending it scurrying for cover with the barking dog in hot pursuit.

Taking people's money—especially lots of money—can be a dangerous occupation. On a trip to Dallas, Thompson set a trap by shooting several poor rounds in the 80s and then offered to play left-handed if given a handicap. A number of local players and onlookers took his bet. He won $5500 on the first day, then gave the boys a chance to win it back. The next day he walked away with over $20,000. That night, a caddie waited for him to come out of a casino and tried to rob him. As mentioned, Thompson was a crack shot; he pulled out the .45 he always carried and killed the caddie with a single shot.

In summer 1966, Thompson showed up at a private course called Horizon Hills in El Paso after hearing that some cotton farmers were looking to bet some big money. Even in his 70s, he still had clear blue eyes and unwrinkled, slender hands. Lee Trevino said he never drove a vehicle; he always showed up in a taxi and left the same way. He never smoked and never drank alcohol.

Thompson joined the club and immediately hit it off with all the local players. Within a week he had taken his new friends for hundreds of dollars playing blackjack, poker and golf (both left- and right-handed). At the end of the week, he was asked nicely to leave.

Thompson lived his final few years in a rest home before passing away in 1974. The story goes that he owned every wheelchair, crutch and cane in the facility and leased them back to the owner for a weekly fee. Apparently he had cleaned up playing checkers.

Gambling Big, Winning Bigger

The heir to Titanic Thompson, Dewey Tomko may make more money than anyone else in golf—Tiger Woods included. He is the world's biggest golf gambler. He has won and lost more than a million dollars in a single round.

In Dewey's world, the rules of golf are catered to meet the gambler's interests. There is no limit on the number of clubs one can carry. Tomko packs 38 clubs into his bag (14 is the limit on the PGA Tour). Some of them he might use only once a year, but any one might save him $50,000 in the right situation. He's got a left-handed tree club and a tiny left-handed club for tight spots, and he packs 11 metal woods to avoid any half shots. He carries seven wedges, one for every five yards.

Tomko also greases up—a layer of Vaseline on the clubface of a driver adds length and accuracy. In any other setting, it's completely illegal, but in gambler's golf there are no out of bounds, no gimmes, no free drops, no handicaps and, if you lean over a ball, even to tie your shoe, you'll lose the hole.

Tomko, now in his 60s, has an old-fashioned crew cut. He only shakes hands with the ends of his fingers, like a piano virtuoso, to protect his most valuable assets. He putts between his legs. And he cleans up when he plays golf against touring pros.

Davis Love III, David Frost, Robert Damron, Paul Azinger, Andy Bean, Fulton Allem and Denis Watson have all lost big money to Tomko. He has a standard bet against the pros—they play from the back tees and Tomko plays from the next set up. They all skip the par fives; they're the holes a professional makes his living on.

Tomko only plays against people who can afford to lose money. He's reportedly taken a lot of Michael Jordan's loot and cleaned up against major league pitcher John Smoltz. In the high-stakes world that Tomko occupies, he most often plays other gamblers.

Golf is only one of his games. By 1982, he was the top-ranked poker player in the world. He has twice finished second at the World Series of Poker. He is also one of the world's largest sports bettors and one of the few who actually makes money at it. He'll bet on almost anything. He won $100,000 by making more free throws wearing cowboy boots and a sport coat than his opponent did wearing a sweat suit.

Tomko has always been a gambler, even when he taught kindergarten in Polk County, Florida. He would stay up late all night, then head to the classroom. At naptime, he would lie down with the kids. It didn't work too well when they couldn't wake him up. Shortly afterward, Tomko headed to Las Vegas for good. It was his calling. He soon started making so much money that he bought his own British-style links course called Southern Dunes.

Over the years, he has played against mobsters, drug dealers, movie stars and the best golf hustlers around. He's put himself in some tight situations against the wrong kind of people. But Tomko has always managed to come out on top. "I just know how to read people," he explains.

Betting Games

Tennison Park in Dallas attracted the poor and the wealthy and the best golf hustlers in North America, including Titanic Thompson, right up to the 1960s, when the PGA circuit started to pay out decent prize money. It was perhaps the most famous municipal course in the world, a rolling layout with two 18-hole courses that featured thousands of pecan trees. During a time when golf was still very much segregated, race, religion and social status didn't matter at Tennison; if you could pay the green fee, you could play.

Golf and guns don't seem to go together, but some courses lack the chic atmosphere of an upscale country club. Lee Trevino loved to play at Tennison and remembered it as a dangerous place that attracted some rough characters. "It was so tough out there that people would skip a stretch of holes away from the clubhouse for fear of getting robbed," recalled Trevino. "One day these two guys are out there playing a match and the bets are flying fast and furious. One guy's out $1000. Just then, these two robbers pop out of the trees with guns. The guy that was losing handed the money to his friend and said, 'We're even.'"

Some of the biggest gamblers in oil-rich Dallas would come out to the course, looking for a new way to lose some money. They would play the "Tunnel Game"—players would bet $25 each, take one club and go out to the farthest point on the golf course. The goal was to hit your ball back to the clubhouse in the fewest strokes by going across the front nine of the east course, first navigating through a concrete tunnel under some railroad tracks. If a player hit over the tunnel, he would have to go back and try again. The tunnel was a narrow, 40-foot walkway—sometimes it took 12 or 13 strokes just to get through.

There was also a game called "Honest John," where players took turns paying every other golfer $10 for every stroke they took to put the ball in the hole. A player having a bad day could lose a lot of money. "Trees" was a variation of Honest John—you paid every other player $10 for each tree you hit. If a ball bounced off one tree and hit another, you paid $20 to each player.

━━ ━━

All golf hustlers have gimmicks. Martin "Fat Man" Stanovich was a golf gambler from Chicago who traveled around the continent looking for big games. The Fat Man was a good player, but he looked terrible on the course. He was about 5 feet, 10 inches tall and 240 pounds. He wore an old, ugly Panama hat that he pulled down on the right side like Al Capone. His swing was awful—his clubs had oversized grips, and he choked down on them. He held the club way out in front of him, and after he hit the ball, he'd fall back on his right foot.

It was mechanically the worst swing around, but it was the Fat Man's gimmick. He would stumble and bumble around the course for a few rounds and, like bees to honey, the bets would come to him. Then he would start to play—it wouldn't look any prettier, but as the round proceeded, the Fat Man would become much wealthier.

These days, talented golfers bypass the hard knocks of the hustling life. Players can make a good living on a number of different golf tours around the world. Gambling, however, is still a popular part of the sport. Some of the games, such as Skins and Stableford, are so accepted that they've become televised packages (Skins games) or have been incorporated into the PGA Tour (Stableford scoring is used in one tour event). There are a number of options for the betting crowd—Nassau, Vegas, Nine Points, Low Total, Wolf, Snake, Instant Replay, Sticks and Bingo, Bango, Bongo. For most of us, a $2 wager will be enough to get the competitive juices flowing; in some parts of Texas, bets under $10,000 are considered an insult.

The British Open Scam

It's not often that a story about golf includes bribery, forgery, fraud and illegal immigration. In 2002, officials at Royal and Ancient Golf Club of St. Andrews accepted $150 entry fees from 47 Nigerians to attend qualifying sessions for the British Open.

Nigeria is hardly a hotbed of golf. Despite having an abundance of oil reserves, most of the country's 126 million people live in poverty. Violence driven by politics, religion and ethnicity has claimed thousands of lives over the years. The economy and education system are in terrible shape. Nigeria lacks even a conventional 18-hole golf course. In the drought-stricken region, the greens are made of sand and oil.

Nigerians are known for their ingenuity in trying to escape their embattled country. This scam was simple, but effective. Each person paid $150 for entry into a qualifying session to the Open in one of 16 sites scattered across Britain and Ireland. Then they applied for a visa to play in the qualifying rounds by paying bribes for forged documents and false affidavits testifying to their intent to play.

At the Hadley Wood Golf Club near London, the check in of players at the first tee began. At 7:30 AM, Martin Yates, an official of the R&A championship committee, called out, "Omoh Ohiro, Nigeria." With no Ohiro in sight, Yates yelled out, "Omoh Ohiro, disqualified."

At 8:55 AM, Yates yelled, "Francis Isuku, Nigeria." A minute later, Yates again, "Isuku, disqualified."

The Open officials were shocked when only four of the 47 Nigerian golfers showed up at their appointed tee time. At first, their concern was that they had gone missing—that they had somehow gotten lost or been kidnapped or met some kind of gruesome fate.

Then as the press began to investigate, it became clear that the Nigerians had come up with an ingenious plan to get into the country.

Fourteen of the 47 had received visas; the other 33 were not approved. Four of the Nigerians were in fact legitimate golfers who showed up at their qualifying event; the other 10 made it to England and then disappeared.

London *Sunday Times* journalist Adrian Turpin summed up the tone of coverage from much of the British media: "Lagos [the capital city of Nigeria] is hardly famed for its rolling links, and to come up with a scheme this ingenious shows exactly the degree of creativity that any nation should surely look for from immigrants."

The St. Andrews officials were embarrassed by the matter and promised they would never let it happen again. They reached an agreement with the Nigerian PGA and the Nigerian Golf Association that all further applications would be checked on the African side first, before being accepted by British golfing authorities. After a formal complaint from the British embassy to the Nigerian authorities, a director of the Nigerian PGA and four players were suspended or expelled.

"It was very, very embarrassing to our association and to our country in general," explained one Nigerian PGA official. "That is why we are taking several steps to see that it does not occur anymore. From now on, no Nigerian will enter the British Open on an individual basis; he must pass through the PGA of Nigeria."

Two months after the Open fiasco, it was reported that 43 Nigerians presented themselves as physicists to receive invitations to a five-day scientific conference in Edinburgh, Scotland. None of them showed up.

The Big Drivers

When John Daly came out of nowhere in 1991 to win the PGA Championship, the long hitter was back in style. After getting into the field as ninth alternate, Daly captured the imagination of golf fans all over the world by throwing caution aside to hit huge drives off the tees. "All four days, I didn't think. I just hit," said Daly after winning the title, "Squeeky [Jeff Medlen, his caddie] said kill it, and I killed it."

In his first nine seasons on the tour, Daly was the unchallenged leader in total driving distance, averaging 306.8 yards per drive in 2002. Since then, a younger generation of bombers led by Hank Kuehne, Bubba Watson and J.B. Holmes has surpassed Daly in distance.

Over the years, the most popular golfers have often been the tour's biggest hitters, starting with Arnold Palmer and continuing with Jack Nicklaus, Johnny Miller, Seve Ballesteros, Greg Norman and Tiger Woods. And though technology and strength training have combined to make the once-impressive 300-yard drive a common feat, there is still something special about a player who can outdistance his rivals with a booming shot off the tee.

The World Long Drive Championship is the Super Bowl for golf's big hitters. Each year, they gather to see who can nail the longest drive. "It's probably the most exciting event in golf," says Jason Zuback, a four-time champion. "It's like a hundred-meter sprint. You're trying to go as fast as you can and hit it by everyone else in the world. It's electrifying, and the crowd really gets into it."

The Long Drivers of America have a mini-tour that culminates in the world championship in a town called Mesquite, about an hour's drive from Las Vegas. More than 5000 spectators trek out to the desert to watch the big hitters take six attempts to whack the ball farther than anyone else, while having to land their shots within a strip 45 yards wide.

Long drivers hit thousands of golf balls each year to learn how to adjust for different weather conditions. Club-head speed, ball spin, trajectory and launch angle all have to be considered to maximize length, depending on what Mother

Nature is up to on a given day. The competitors all use specialized shafts, club heads and grips to squeeze out the extra yards required to qualify with the best hitters.

The winner takes home $80,000, with the title also opening up the lucrative world of sponsorship and exhibitions. Champions can earn in excess of $500,000 per year in winnings, endorsements and demonstrations. Of the 96 golfers (out of about 14,000) who qualify for the world championship, only the top 12 to 15 hitters can make a good living showing off their skills at exhibitions and corporate events.

Zuback, a Calgary, Alberta, pharmacist, won the 1997 contest with a 412-yard drive, and his personal best is 511 yards. He also bounced a drive 714 yards down an airport runway. He charges $7500 a day for his services and has driven golf balls through pumpkins, watermelons, particle board, department store mannequins and telephone books. It's all part of his routine.

Kelly Murray, a Vancouver long-hitter, was on the front pages of local newspapers when he whacked a shot 422 yards off the roof of the Pan Pacific Hotel in his hometown. Sometimes he's asked to hit balls across rivers. He can cream a ball 300 yards on his knees.

Many long-shot specialists follow various golf tours, giving exhibitions at event stops while trying to qualify for the tournaments. The income from the demonstrations helps ease the financial pressure of life on the road.

However, most of the big hitters lack the shot-making and putting skills to make money on professional tours. Players such as Zuback and world champion Sean "The Beast" Fister have stopped worrying about tournament golf; instead, they entertain hundreds of people each year by hitting a golf ball a mile.

The Trick-Shot Artists

The most famous golfing-related television commercial involved a trick shot from some guy named Tiger Woods. Do you remember the 1999 Nike ad that shows Tiger bouncing a golf ball on the face of his wedge while passing the club from hand to hand and between his legs and behind his back before hitting the ball out of the air and down the fairway?

That wildly successful commercial was never planned. Woods was between takes on a shoot for another Nike ad when, to pass the time, he began doing the stunt that he had taught himself as a kid.

Woods explained that the trick evolved when, as a youngster, he spent hours waiting between holes on par-three courses. "To kill the time, some of the guys and I started playing with hacky sacks, kicking them around, and then we started bouncing balls on our golf clubs. Next thing you know, we started doing tricks and playing catch and running on the tee boxes and just having a whole bunch of fun playing catch."

There is a small group of professional golfers who make most of their money as trick-shot art-ists—a golf bag jammed with crazy-looking clubs is one tip off that one is close by. They are golf's version of the circus clown. The organizers of golf tournaments and trade shows hire players such as Sandy Kurceba to entertain. Kurceba, a former player on the Canadian, Australian and senior tours, carries two-headed irons and driv-ers, a whip-like driver, a wacky wedge and a driver on the end of a hose in his oversized golf bag. He'll hit shots wearing hockey skates off oversized tees and pop bottles.

And then there's the always crowd-pleasing, hit-a-ball-teed-up-on-a-person's-face shot. "I tee the ball pretty high on that one because I think the liability would be pretty high," said Kurceba, who considers himself a showman with a good golf game.

Dennis Walters became a trick-shot artist after misfortune ended his dream of becoming a golf pro. In 1976, Walters was in a golf cart accident that left him without feeling or movement in his legs. After suffering through months of hospitalization and therapy, the Florida resident began hitting golf balls from his wheelchair.

Walters was desperate to find a way to get involved in the sport he loved. A friend adapted a swivel chair to a golf cart, allowing Walters to take some full swings. He started fooling around with some trick shots and, after much practice, decided to take his show on the road.

Walters has performed thousands of times at tournaments and charity events. He can hit amazingly precise drives of over 200 yards and chips and putts one-handed. At the same time, Walters slips some inspired words into his program to remind the audience that perseverance and hard work can overcome almost any obstacle.

Chapter Six

Blow-ups, Dust-ups, Dress-ups and Pin-ups

The great Bobby Jones once said, "Golf is a game that creates emotions that sometimes cannot be sustained with a club in the hand." Golf has been called the most frustrating game. The craft of hitting a small ball into a slightly larger hole has temporarily turned the most levelheaded, intelligent individuals into raging lunatics.

Anger Management

The very best golfers are not immune to the mental pitfalls of the sport. Let's start with Davis Love III—maybe not the happiest looking guy on the circuit, but usually he keeps it together. In 1999, he became upset after hitting a poor shot at the Bay Hill Invitational, the tournament that Arnold Palmer hosts each year.

Love took an angry swipe with his sand wedge and hit a sprinkler head. The sprinkler started sprinkling and didn't stop. The par-three 17th hole began to flood. Crews had to be called in to clean up the mess. After the tourney ended, Love received a bill from Palmer for the damage: $3.50 for the new sprinkler head, $175,000 for the labor required to dry out the hole.

Curtis Strange gained a reputation as the most intense player on the PGA Tour. His temper reached a new zenith in 1982 after he hit an errant shot at the Doral-Eastern Open Invitational. The poor shot set off a bout of temporary insanity. Strange booted his golf bag while it was on the shoulder of his caddie, Gene Kelley. The kick knocked the caddie down, and three weeks later he had surgery to fuse two of his vertebrae. Kelley hired an attorney, and his boss settled out of court, agreeing to pay for the medical expenses and throwing in a small amount of cash.

Two years earlier, Strange had managed to hold his displeasure in check after disaster struck before the last hole of the second round of the Inverrary Classic. Strange had struggled and needed par on the 18th to make the cut. As he and his caddie made their way across a narrow bridge, a spectator jostled his golf bag. The caddie lost control, and one by one the clubs began sliding into the deep water below.

Strange managed to grab the caddie and the golf bag, but the only clubs left were a two iron, a three iron, a five iron and a putter. He took stock and hit a solid two iron off the tee, followed up with a long five iron onto the green and then two-putted. He made the cut, hired a local diver to retrieve his clubs and was back in action the next morning.

━ ━

At the 1992 Los Angeles Open, Mark Calcavec-chia slammed his club onto a cart path after a lousy drive. The shaft literally exploded, and pieces of it barely missed a nearby spectator.

━ ━

And then there's the case of a fan taking out a player. At the World Series of Golf in 1994, John Daly launched one of his patented drives before letting the group ahead of him clear out. The "Wild Thing" was having a bad day (he would finish with a round of 83) and was play-ing fast. A club pro named Jeffrey Roth barely moved out of the way to avoid having Daly's ball tattooed into his body.

After the round, Roth's mother and Daly exchanged words in the parking lot. Roth's 62-year-old father didn't like what was being said and jumped Daly from behind. Daly suffered a back injury during the altercation and was forced to sit out the rest of the season.

━ ━

Tommy Bolt's nicknames were "Thunder Bolt" and "Terrible Tommy." Both were in reference to his temper on the course. At the 1960 U.S. Open, he hit two drives into the water on the 18th hole at Denver's Cherry Hills Country Club. After the second shot, Bolt hurled his driver into the pond, too. A famous photograph of his over-the-shoulder release of the club became a celebrated image of golf at its most frustrating.

A young boy dived into the pond and came out with the driver. Bolt approached the boy with his money clip in hand to show his appreciation. He never got the chance to pay. The kid took off with the club, raced through the gallery and jumped over a fence.

Later, Bolt insisted he had never meant to throw his club in the water. "It was just a hot day and those worn grips got a little slick on Old Tom," he recalls. "Hell, I was just taking a practice swing for myself, and the next thing I knew that little beauty was sailing out over the water. It was a shame—I really liked that club too."

Another story, perhaps slightly exaggerated, has Bolt at a tournament facing a 120-yard shot to the green at the final hole. His caddie handed him a three iron.

"What the hell is this, son?" he asked. "I can hit this club almost 200 yards."

"I know, sir," his caddie said. "But it's the only iron you have left. You broke all the rest."

Bolt claimed that he never threw as many clubs as people claimed, but he does admit that he taught Arnold Palmer how to do it properly. "I had to take the boy aside and teach him how to throw a club," said Bolt, the winner of 15 PGA titles, including the 1958 U.S. Open. "He was so innocent he'd toss them backwards. I had to explain that you'd get worn out walking back to pick them up. You have to throw them in front of you if you're going to be a professional."

During the final round of the 2002 Pebble Beach Pro-Am, Pat Perez blew a gasket. At the par-five 14th hole, he first made two wild swings with his three wood and then pounded it into the sod. Amazingly, he held it together enough to reclaim the tournament lead until he reached the par-five 18th. He hit his drive out of bounds by inches, then sailed his fourth shot into the

Pacific Ocean, then tried to break his poor three wood over his knee.

▬ ◀

Craig Stadler was never one to hide his emotions on the golf course. The "Walrus" was playing a par-three in the final round of the 1985 Hawaiian Open when he hit his tee shot into a bunker. Frustrated, Stadler took a swipe at one of the pineapple tee markers, which he assumed were plastic. His club made contact with the marker, which happened to be a real pineapple. The marker exploded, spraying sauce-like goop everywhere. The mishap seemed to break the tension, and Stadler shot a 64 to finish second.

▬ ◀

John Huston provided one of the golf's funniest images at the 1992 Honda Classic. During the first round, he hooked two drives into the lake on the par-five seventh hole. His next drive went way right, and Huston decided the club was to blame. He whirled his Wilson Whale driver into the lake that took his first two balls. When the club floated to the surface, he went after it. Wading into the water, Huston didn't know there was drop-off. Suddenly, he vanished; only his hat was visible on the surface. Huston gained a new nickname out of the soggy experience: "Swamp Thing."

The Man of Many Excesses

He may be more popular than Tiger Woods, and several of his fellow pros, including Tiger, believe he is the most talented player in golf. He is golf's greatest character and one of the sport's biggest draws.

In 1991, a big, blonde-haired kid from Arkansas burst onto the scene with a victory at the PGA Championship. John Daly instantly became a crowd favorite, awing fellow pros and fans alike with his monster drives and go-for-it-all attitude. The legend of Daly has grown over the years, full of stories of excess (tobacco, booze, women, gambling, food) mixed with greatness (one of only six golfers to win two major titles by the age of 30).

From his own book, *My Life in and out of the Rough*, Daly throws out some amazing numbers for the reader to ponder. First there was the 18 he scored on the sixth hole of the Bay Hill Invitational in 1998. How do you score an 18, especially after you hit a good drive on the par-five sixth hole? Answer: pull out a three wood and try a 270-yard approach shot to a green that's guarded by a lake. Six straight times, Daly tried that shot. After each of the first five attempts there was a splash—and five penalty shots—and on the sixth he buried the ball into a bunker.

Follow up with four more shots to the green and two putts, and it adds up to 18.

After finishing the round with an 85, Daly summed up his strategy: "It wasn't that I didn't care. I just lost my patience. I was determined. I knew the shot. I had the courage to try it. I just didn't have the wisdom to bail out. The way I look at it, it's progress before perfection. I'm not going to worry about it. I just got a hell of a lot of practice with my three wood."

The Bay Hill disaster was only one of several Daly-sized blow-ups. At the British Open the same year, he needed only a bogey on the 18th hole to make the cut. Instead he took a 10, including five shots out of a fairway bunker. The next year, he six-putted on the 18th to take another 10 at the Memorial in Dublin, Ohio. Just over two weeks later at the U.S. Open, Daly fell apart again. After shooting an opening round of 69, only a shot out of the lead, he chipped back and forth across the par-four eighth hole to score an 11, missing the cut with an 83. Afterward, he said he'd no longer play in the Open.

In 2000, Daly changed his mind and played the U.S. Open at Pebble Beach in California. In his first round he shot a 14 on the par-five 18th—pumping one tee shot out of bounds to the right before hooking two more into the ocean. After shooting an 83, Daly withdrew from the tournament.

Daly will never be a poster boy for moderation. The numbers he's put up in his private life are also big.

Tobacco: Daly likes to smoke during tournaments. By his own estimation, he goes through 14,600 Marlboro Lights per year (about two packs a day). A Daly trademark is a cigarette dangling from his mouth between holes.

Diet: Daly has topped the scales at over 290 pounds and once lost 65 pounds in three months. He remains a big eater with a penchant for Diet Coke—an estimated 15 cans a day, or just over 500 gallons a year.

Alcohol: As a college freshman, he was told to lose weight or he wouldn't get to play for the golf team. Daly's diet consisted of cigarettes, Jack Daniels whisky and a bit of popcorn. He dropped the pounds, but was soon in the hospital after passing out from alcohol poisoning. Daly has battled the bottle for years and has had two rehab stints.

Gambling: In perhaps his most shocking revelation, Daly estimates he's lost about $55 million in the last 15 years. He makes between 30 and 40 trips to casinos each year and has gambled away his tournament paycheck in one day.

Women: He penned a country tune called "All My Exes Wear Rolexes" in honor of his four marriages. One of his wives, Sherrie Daly, was convicted and sentenced to five months in prison for her role in a money-laundering scheme. His yearly alimony bill is in the hundreds of thousands of dollars.

Travel: Daly hates flying, so he spent $1.5 million on a custom designed motor home to travel between tour stops. The RV is 950 square feet inside with a king-sized bed, two 42-inch plasma TVs, a full kitchen, a washer-dryer and a full bathroom. He puts on about 35,000 miles each year and makes some money on the side by hawking merchandise such as beer mugs, caps and T-shirts out of a trailer he pulls behind.

Some of the sport's biggest names—Arnold Palmer, Jack Nicklaus, Tom Watson and Greg Norman—have tried to help him through the many turbulent times over the years. Even as Daly's golf game has slid, his popularity remains undiminished. He commands top dollars in appearance fees to attend Skins games and other made-for-TV events. At least a few times each season, he regains some of his magic and contends for a title.

The People's Golfer

Lee Trevino grew up the hard way in Dallas, in severe poverty, and he never knew who his father was. His mother raised the family in a four-room shack with no plumbing, electricity or even windows; the kitchen had a dirt floor.

Somehow he made his way to a golf course and found his passion—and a way out. It wasn't an easy journey. Much of his game was self-taught. He didn't get to college. He learned the game on the rock-hard fairways of Texas. He was a member of the grounds crew, he caddied and he found the time to hit thousands of golf balls, and eventually he became a club professional. On the course, he hustled bets to supplement his meager salary. It took him a while to make the PGA Tour, but a win at the 1968 U.S. Open solidified his standing. He knew he belonged, and he developed into one of the most consistent and popular players on the circuit, winning 29 PGA events and another 29 on the Seniors Tour.

He never forgot his hard start in life. On the course, he always seemed to be having fun. He genuinely liked talking to the fans during a round. He was once asked about the pressures of playing tournament golf, especially in a major. Trevino put the game in context with his reply:

"Pressure is playing for ten dollars when you don't have a dime in your pocket."

Trevino won three out of the four major tournaments in his illustrious career (six majors in all), but the Masters eluded him. The course wasn't built for his game—Trevino was a technician, a precise shot-maker who relied on accuracy.

The short rough at Augusta National allows the long hitter to bomb away. Trevino dared to publicly criticize the layout of the course. He backed up his words in 1970 and 1971 by refusing his invitation to play in the event. He did return reluctantly and without success. But in 1984, he was in trouble with the Masters brass again during the third round of play.

It had rained throughout the afternoon, and by the time the group Trevino was playing with made the 16th green, the putting surface was saturated with water. The other members of the threesome, George Archer and David Graham, played their putts even though the entire hole was covered with water.

The Masters officials were trying to keep the tournament on schedule for television purposes, so Sunday's round would start on time. When it was Trevino's turn to putt, he called an official over and told him the hole was unplayable. The official looked at him and said, "Well, you have to putt," to which Trevino replied, "If you think I'm going to putt, you better call the clubhouse and get your lunch; we're going to be out here for a while."

Phone calls were made until finally Clyde Mangum, the deputy commissioner of the PGA Tour, was contacted. The Masters officials pleaded their case, but admitted the hole was surrounded by water. Mangum told the course marshals to squeegee the green, and Trevino received a standing ovation from the 15,000-member gallery.

After the hole was finally dried out, Trevino rubbed salt in the wounds by dragging his club behind him as he walked to the next hole. Water splashed up from the club head, showing television viewers the bad shape the course was in.

Casey Martin Fights On

Sometimes the rigidity of tradition makes the keepers of golf look like knuckleheads. Take the case of Casey Martin, a young pro with a rare leg disorder who must rely on a golf cart to make it through a round. Did the PGA embrace the idea of someone with a disability fighting through multiple obstacles to join the best golfers in the world? Did they try to make things easier for him—to accommodate his physical handicap so he could play with the big boys?

No. Instead, the PGA said that it had the right to make its own rules and that walking was an integral part of the game. They said that if they let Martin ride, they'd have to do the same for every other pro who claimed an injury or illness.

Their position was wacky—especially when the PGA-run Champions Tour allows carts for its tournaments, qualifying school and to transport players from certain tees to greens. Martin was forced to take the PGA to court, where he won rulings in both Oregon and the Supreme Court.

It was a long road for the kid with the wholesome American looks. Martin was born with a rare disorder called Klippel-Trenaunay-Weber Syndrome. The veins in one of his legs leak internally, causing swelling and pain. Because the bone is soaked all the time, it becomes brittle.

He was a sports nut as a kid, playing basketball and football, but the toll of those sports on his leg led him to switch to golf, using a cart. After a successful college career at Stanford, where he was part of the school's 1994 NCAA championship team, Martin joined the Nike Tour (now the Buy.com Tour). In 1998, he won a tournament and finished in the top 15 on the money list, which qualified him to play on the PGA Tour, all on less than two legs.

His wonderful expectations of playing in the big league turned into a disaster. The world found out about his disability and the golf cart. Everyone had an opinion—each tour stop was a circus, and Martin's play suffered. He ended up 179th on the money list and was once again relegated to the minors.

It's a miracle that he can make it through a round of golf at all, let alone compete at a high level. He takes 12 to 14 Advil a day—he can only sleep in two-hour shifts before he needs to dull the pain. He has to wear two nylon restraining stockings on his leg to keep the swelling down. He takes huge risks with every round—a fall could break a bone in his fragile leg. A break below the knee would mean amputation. Other golf pros say he has almost perfect balance in his swing, something Martin had to develop to take pressure off his hurting leg.

And yet, every step of the way, the PGA has thrown obstacles in his path. They created a whole rule-book on how he could and could not use the cart: the caddie can't drive; the bag can't go inside; the cart can't have a roof (an unfair advantage, they claim, to have shade from the sun or shelter from the rain); no personal stuff is allowed in the cart—not even a tee in a tee holder; and he may not ride ahead of the walking players.

After the Supreme Court ruled in his favor in 2002, Martin almost made it back to the PGA Tour. At the qualifying tournament at the tough PGA West Course in La Quinta, California, he was 21st heading into the final day. He needed to stay in the top 35 to earn his playing card. Two double bogeys on the 13th and 14th holes were his undoing, as Martin shot a 77 and missed his card by three shots.

Martin returned to the Nike Tour in 2003 but was relegated to part-time status in 2004. He had only limited status again in 2005, but with a sponsor's exemption was able to play at the AT&T PGA event at Pebble Beach. He made the cut and finished 65th. In 2006, he was able to play only five nationwide events. The same year, he was named head coach of the University of Oregon's men's golf team. He still dreams about making it back to the PGA Tour but did not play in any professional events in 2007.

Blind Betting

In 1941, Charley Boswell was a top baseball prospect, a gifted athlete who had played football as a tailback with Crimson Tide at the University of Alabama. He decided to postpone his baseball career when he joined the U.S. army in 1941.

On November 30, 1944, a German artillery shell blinded Boswell. It exploded just after he had rescued his friend from a tank that was under fire. While recovering at a rehabilitation hospital in Philadelphia, he took up golf for the first time—blind golfers play with the aid of a caddy or sight coach, who helps direct their shots.

Boswell's natural athletic abilities carried over to his new sport. Over the next 23 years, he won 28 national and international tournaments for blind golfers, including 16 U.S. Blind Golf Championships. Along the way, he found the time to start an insurance company, raise a family and serve as Alabama's state revenue commissioner.

His golfing exploits (he once shot an 81) brought Boswell considerable fame. He became friends with Alan Shepard, Ken Venturi, Bob Hope and several PGA pros. In 1958, he won the Ben Hogan Award for his dedication to the game, and it was arranged that he would play a round with the great golf champion.

Boswell was awestruck about meeting his hero, and perhaps out of nervousness, challenged Hogan to play for money. The best pro golfer of his era deftly sidestepped the challenge, but the blind champion persisted and raised the stakes to $1000 a hole.

"I can't, what would people think of me, taking advantage of you and your circumstance," replied Hogan.

Boswell then called Hogan a chicken. Finally, the bet was agreed to, and an angered Hogan warned Boswell that he would play his best and asked him to name the time and the place for the round to begin, to which Boswell cheekily replied, "10 o'clock tonight."

Both Boswell and Hogan shared a big laugh and then had a great afternoon on the course. It was Boswell's outgoing personality that made him a favorite of the rich and famous. He used those skills to great purpose in establishing a celebrity golf event that, over the years that it was held, raised $1.5 million for the Eye Foundation Hospital. Boswell died in 1995 at the age of 78.

Funky Fashion

Until his tragic death in a plane crash in 1999, Payne Stewart was in a league by himself when it came to style on the PGA Tour. He was a heck of a golfer too. His smooth, effortless swing won him the 1989 PGA Championship and a pair of U.S. Open titles (1991, 1999).

Stewart was one of most charismatic players on the tour. He was equally popular with fans and the other players. He played harmonica in a rock band called Jake Trout and the Flounders, which also featured fellow pro Peter Jacobsen.

The Stewart trademark, however, was the vintage-type clothing he wore on the tour. With the knickers and the Hogan-style tam-o'-shanter caps, he looked like a character out of an F. Scott Fitzgerald novel. He caused a fuss at the 1987 Masters (a tournament he never really liked) by choosing pink knickers, a white dress shirt, a pink bow tie and pink knee socks with polka dots.

In 1988, the NFL approached him with a promotional deal. For a good sum of money, Stewart wore the colors of the NFL team closest to the location of the tournament he was playing in during a particular week. It was the first time a major active player in one sport had become an official spokesperson for another sport.

At the Colonial National Invitational in Fort Worth, Texas, Stewart had some fun with his new role. In the middle of Dallas Cowboy football territory, he wore the colors of the Washington Redskins—the Cowboys' hated rival. For the final round, he switched to Cowboy colors to let the fans know he was just fooling around.

Stewart actually wore long pants the first couple of years he was on the tour, but a European player named Stewart Ginn gave him the idea of switching to knickers. It was a way of setting himself apart from the other players. He became known for his outgoing personality and his unique sense of style. During the 1990s, he was one of the most recognizable players in the game.

At the height of his popularity and golfing success, Stewart and two business associates, plus a pilot and co-pilot, died when something went wrong in the Learjet 35 they had chartered to look at a site for a new golf course. A sudden depressurization due to an oxygen leak was the suspected cause of the mishap. Their plane flew unguided until it ran out of fuel, then crashed in a South Dakota field. Stewart was only 42.

Although Stewart was the trailblazer on the PGA Tour when it came to retro clothing, it took a Swede to modernize fashion on the men's side. At the 1997 Bob Hope Classic, Jesper Parnevik, who was known for flipping up the bill of his cap while he played, showed up at the tournament in an ensemble of bright, tight-fitting clothes from Swedish designer Johan Lindeberg.

It was a huge shift in style. In the 1990s, black, navy and khaki were the dominant colors on the circuit. This boring attire contrasted with the garishness of the 1980s, when the men wore badly matched bright colors and plaids. Back then, golf had a reputation for having badly dressed men hitting a little white ball. Comedian Robin Williams summed up golf attire at the time: "Golf is a game where white men can dress up as black pimps and get away with it." Things became much more conservative in the '90s— solid pants and solid shirts.

Parnevik changed that in a hurry. At one tournament he wore aqua pants, a white belt and a bright turquoise shirt with orange down the side. He became a trailblazer for individualism.

A lot of pros have followed Parnevik and taken fashion risks. Darren Clarke showed up at a tournament dressed in bright orange from head to toe. He has a personal tailor in London who supplies him with pants that grab attention in colors such as mustard yellow, kelly green and black with gold glitter.

Ian Poulter also wanted to take some blandness out of the tour. He was on the front of sports pages around Europe and North America when he played in the British Open with a Union Jack pattern on his pants. A couple of months later at the PGA Championship, he was adorned with the Stars and Stripes.

Many of the younger stars are now having some fun with their golf wardrobe. Scott Hend wore bright yellow pants and a kelly green shirt at Torrey Pines, and Hunter Mahan has worn pink pants and a matching hat at several events. Charles Howell III wore white pants with a green stripe down the side at the Masters. Aaron Baddeley was given the nickname "Dresses" (as in dresses badly) after showing up on tour with tight-fitting short sleeve shirts and a white belt.

These days, Parnevik hardly stands out. Golfers are dressed in all types of fits and colors. It's easy to forget how much style on the tour has evolved over the last 10 years. "I never felt like a pioneer," said Parnevik. "I didn't think it would come this far, where you see everybody going in that direction. I didn't think it would be this fast. But it's fun."

▬ ◅

Sometimes there is a fine line between the outrageous and the ill chosen. At the 2006 British Open, Sergio Garcia was in contention to win his first major championship. The 26-year-old

Spaniard had crafted a marvelous third-round 65 to trail Tiger Woods by only one stroke. In the final round, Garcia was paired with Woods and showed up that day wearing a garish bright yellow outfit.

On two of the first three holes, Garcia missed short par putts. Woods began to leave the rest of the field behind in winning his third British Open title. Garcia not only shot a final round 73 to slip to fifth, but the press had a lot of fun at his expense. The young Spaniard was called a canary and a lemon. And Woods, well, he wore his trademark red shirt for the final round and walked off the course with another major title. Nobody was criticizing his fashion sense.

Sex Sells

A reporter once asked Babe Didrikson Zaharias, women's golf's first star player, how she could hit a golf ball 250 yards wearing the constraining clothes that were in style. She replied quite candidly, "You've got to loosen your girdle and let it rip."

Over the years, the LPGA has struggled to be as forthright on what kind of image it wants players to project. Popular professionals such as Kathy Whitworth, Nancy Lopez and Judy Rankin were role models in the traditional sense—they were top players who had solid marriages and nice-looking kids.

In the mid-1980s, an Australian player named Jan Stephenson took the women's tour to new levels of popularity with a different approach. Stephenson had blonde pin-up looks, and she openly embraced her sex appeal to sell the game. She became famous outside the boundaries of the sport when she posed in a bathtub—covered up only by golf balls. She later posed in a pin-up calendar that sold in the hundreds of thousands.

The big hair, bright makeup and glamorous outfits were in sharp contrast to the values promoted by the leaders of the feminist movement, which was highly influential at the time. Sports had a high profile, and feminist leaders wanted female athletes to be respected and compensated on an equal footing with their male counterparts. The only problem was that the women's game has never had access to the same money that was thrown around on the men's side. The purses were smaller; the galleries were smaller; there were fewer televised tournaments; and corporate support was lacking.

Stephenson believed that the attractive stars on their circuit should be showcased. "We have to promote sex appeal. It's a fact of life. The people who watch are predominantly male, and they won't keep watching if the girls aren't beautiful."

Fortunately for the LPGA, Stephenson had credibility because she was a talented golfer. She had 16 tour victories, including three major championships. She also helped found the Women's Seniors Golf Tour and became the first woman to play on the men's Champions Tour (formerly the Seniors Tour).

In 2005, the LPGA launched a full-fledged campaign to promote their attractive players, regardless of their standing on the tour. Rookies were showcased as prominently as established stars.

Now women's golf has a new pin-up girl named Natalie Gulbis. She's a good player, but most of her popularity stems from her beauty and her outgoing personality. She has modeled for five swimsuit calendars. She's done two pictorials for men's magazines and has been named one of the world's 100 sexiest women. She's even had her own reality show on the Golf Channel.

Gulbis tops a list of attractive young women who are starting to build name recognition for the LPGA. Michelle Wie has struggled to find her game, yet she has the potential to become the best player on the women's circuit. Paula Creamer has risen up the money list while making a striking fashion statement with her head-to-toe pink outfits. Mexico's Lorena Ochoa set a new single-season money record in 2007 while wearing super-flared pants.

More people are watching women's golf. Cute girls with athletic physiques and sassy attitudes have led to a jump in the TV ratings. The golf skirts and shorts are riding lower on the hips and higher on the thighs. The shirts are shorter and more formfitting. Although pushing dress codes to the limit, these young women are also talented players.

The once-ostracized Stephenson (who is now called "Nana" by some of the younger players) says the strong feminist subtext that she battled has now been replaced by a freedom that allows these women to be themselves. "In my day, we were fighting for the fact that we were professional athletes," said golf's first pin-up girl. "Nowadays, if you've got it all, you need to flaunt it to make money."

Chapter Seven

Infamous Collapses and Silly Mistakes

Tournament golf. It's nothing like playing a round with your friends. Does your heart beat a little faster on the first tee when you're being watched, not just by your buddies, but by the next few groups, the people eating lunch on the clubhouse patio and maybe the kid running the pro shop who you know can kill the ball?

Now, how about hitting a shot with thousands of people watching you—not just at the first tee box, but for the next 18 holes—or putting up with the roar of the crowd at some distant fairway just as you're about to swing.

No, tournament golf is not like golfing with your friends. Imagine having to sink a four-foot putt knowing that if you don't put it in, you don't make the cut and if you don't make the cut, you don't make any money and if you don't make any money, you don't stay on the tour and if you don't stay on the tour, you might be back home trying to straighten some duffer's hook.

In tournament golf, you have to be able to hit the ball a long way. There are no short holes—unless they're deceptively sinister. If you miss the 25-yard-wide fairway, you're in rough designed to do evil things with your club head as you come through the ball.

In tournament golf, the greens are nothing like a public course. The pin is never in the middle—three paces from the edge is the usual standard. A slight misjudgment, and the next shot is a chip out of the rough or a sand shot out of the bunker. They are all hard and fast. They have 180-degree breaks. They are built into hills where an off-line putt will take your ball into a water hazard. Approach shots have to be almost perfect to stick on the sheer surface.

Tournament golf is designed to expose weaknesses and wear down the mind and the body. In major tournaments (the U.S. Open, the Masters, the British Open and the PGA Championship) the pressure is amplified even more. All of this pressure has led to some memorable collapses, often by the best players. Sometimes it's so disastrous that it's hard to watch.

The Shark's Demise at the 1996 Masters

Greg Norman had the whole golf package that made him one of the tour's most popular players: a fearless go-for-the-pin style, good looks, the perfect nickname and respect from his fellow touring pros. For over 10 years, he won a lot of titles and a lot of money. But for all his success,

Norman had no luck in major tournaments—only one victory (a British Open title) despite holding third-round leads seven times.

Fate had been especially unkind to him at the Masters. In 1986, he was the guy that bogeyed the last hole, allowing Jack Nicklaus to clinch his final and most emotional major victory. The next year, Larry Mize sank a chip shot in a playoff to deny Norman again.

By 1996, Norman was a sentimental favorite to win a major, any major. That year at Augusta National, the Shark opened with a course-record–tying 63, and by the end of the third round, he had built a six-shot lead over Nick Faldo. It seemed at last that Norman was going to win on a course that rewards bold play.

The cruelty of golf was never more evident in what must have been the longest day in Greg Norman's life. On the first hole, Norman pushed a seven-foot par putt to the right—the lead was down to five.

On the fourth hole, a par-three, he pushed his tee shot into the front bunker and failed to get up and down; Faldo shot par—the lead was down to four.

On the sixth hole, Faldo birdied, making a quick recovery from a bogey on the fifth—the lead was still four.

On the seventh hole, Norman missed a 10-foot birdie putt that would have changed the momentum—the lead was still four.

On the par-five eighth, Norman began to do everything the experts on TV said he shouldn't. A wildly pulled fairway wood second shot led to a clutch recovery out of the rough that landed close enough to the green to chip in to save par, but Faldo birdied—the lead was down to three.

On the ninth, Norman had a 100-yard wedge shot to the green. The safe play was to aim the ball long. Norman's ball landed short and rolled slowly, agonizingly, all the way back down the huge hill in front of the green. He bogeyed, paring his lead to two.

Disaster continued on the 10th hole. His approach to the flagstick went left of the green, and his chip ran 12 feet past the hole. Norman missed the putt left—his lead was down to one shot heading into the famous Amen Corner. By this time, the television announcers were saying that Norman was in big trouble and noted that no one had ever blown a final round lead of more than five shots.

On the 11th, he hit a terrific putt that took a look at the hole but missed on the high side before stopping nearly four feet past the hole. Norman took a long time over his par putt, then missed it to the right for his third-straight bogey; Faldo tapped in for par—both players were tied at nine-under.

A visibly stunned Norman then faced the hardest shot at Augusta. On the 12th tee, players must carry a middle bunker 155 yards to safely land on the green. "Picture your target," caddie Tony Navarro told him. "Just over the bunker." Norman fired at the pin, but his ball landed short and rolled back into the water; Faldo hit the green. Norman made double bogey; Faldo made par—Faldo was in the lead by two.

On the 13th, Norman's drive soared wide right, and he was forced to lay-up. Faldo put more pressure on the Shark by two-putting for a birdie, but Norman matched him with a 15-footer for birdie. The crowd erupted, trying to will the Aussie to keep fighting—Faldo still led by two.

On the 15th, Norman hit what appeared to be a perfect eagle chip, but the ball didn't fall. Both players made birdies—Faldo's lead remained at two shots.

On the 16th, Norman hit his worst shot of the day—a hacker's pull-hook from the tee that landed in the middle of the pond. The deal was sealed; Faldo was ahead by four.

On the 18th, the crowd cheered in sympathy for Norman as he walked down the fairway to the final green. The Shark was like a dead man walking. Some spectators actually looked down, hoping not to make eye contact.

Faldo rolled in a meaningless 20-footer for birdie, a five-shot victory and his third Masters title. After hugging his caddie, Faldo fished his ball out of the hole. He turned to Norman and gave him a long hug. "I don't know what to say. I just want to give you a hug. I feel horrible about what happened. I'm so sorry." Both men teared up.

"Yeah, I know I screwed up," Norman said afterward about his final round 78. "But it's not the end of the world for me. I'm disappointed. I'm sad about it. I'm going to regret it. But I'm not going to fall off the face of the earth because of what's happened. It's not going to affect my life. Please believe me.

"All these hiccups I have, they must be for a reason. All this is just a test. I just don't know what the test is yet."

It turned out to be the last real chance that the Shark had to win at Augusta. In 1997, Tiger Woods established a new 72-hole scoring record in his first appearance at the Masters. A new era had begun.

Burned at the British Open

Only the most rabid golf fan would have known who Jean Van de Velde was before the 1999 British Open. A regular on the European Tour, Van de Velde played brilliantly for 71 holes and, heading to the 18th tee, had a three-shot lead at the Carnoustie Golf Club.

The engraver was nearly finished etching Van de Velde's name onto the champion's trophy when the Frenchman stepped into the tee box to hit his drive on the 487-yard final hole. The ball went well right and came to rest on the 17th fairway. Between his ball and the flagstick lay Barry Burn, a serpentine-shaped body of water that is one of most feared hazards on the course. Luckily, Van de Velde had a good lie and, taking out a two iron, decided to go for the green.

Van de Velde's second shot also headed right, clearing the burn but hitting the grandstand. The ball ricocheted off the bleachers, missed the burn coming back but landed in tall grass about 30 yards short of the green. This time the ball was buried. On his next swing, the ball popped out of the rough but dribbled into the water.

Van de Velde took off his shoes and socks, rolled up his trousers and waded into the burn. A famous photo shows him standing in the ankle-high water, hands on his hips, trying to figure out what to do. Lying three already, Van de Velde was faced with an almost impossible shot—hit out of water, clear a very close concrete wall and then land the ball softly enough for it to stay on the green.

Instead of attempting the risky shot, Van de Velde opted to take a penalty stroke and drop outside the hazard. His fifth shot into a greenside bunker didn't make things easier. His bunker shot left him six feet from the pin. From holding a three-shot lead, Van de Velde now needed to sink the putt to qualify for a playoff with Paul Lawrie and Justin Leonard. He held his nerves, and the putt went in.

A four-hole playoff is used to break ties at the British Open. Lawrie, who shot a 67 the last round, had trailed Van de Velde by 10 shots and never believed he still had a shot at the title. Leonard had bogeyed the final hole and never considered the possibility of making a playoff. Over the four-hole tiebreaker, Lawrie was the steadiest player, shooting par to win the championship.

Unfortunately for Lawrie, the 1999 British Open is remembered more for how it was lost. Like Greg Norman three years earlier, Van de Velde faced the golf media after losing the playoff and patiently answered their questions. "It's a game," he told them. "There are worse things in life."

Lefty Leaves a Gift

Heading into the 2006 U.S. Open at Winged Foot, Phil Mickelson was on a roll. The left-hander, who for many years held the title as the best player to have never won a major, captured the 2004 and 2006 Masters and the 2005 PGA Championship. Many golfing pundits were stating that Mickelson had emerged to become a true rival for Tiger Woods.

The West Course at Winged Foot Golf Club in Mamaroneck, New York, had played especially tough for the championship. Winged Foot has hosted many memorable Opens, including Hale Irwin's seven-over-par triumph in 1974 that is remembered as "the Massacre." At the time, many members of the media claimed that the USGA's championship committee had made the course too difficult.

Sandy Tatum, the committee chairman, was asked if the committee was trying to embarrass the best players in the world. "No, we're trying to identify them," shot back Tatum.

Besides the thick rough and the relentlessly long par fours, Winged Foot features glassy, slick greens that are left to dry out in the New York heat. For most of the tournament's four days, Mickelson had survived all the tests the course had to offer to stand at four over par with one hole to play.

Lefty had only a one-shot lead on Geoff Ogilvy heading to the par-four 18th. Mickelson had struggled with his driver all day, hitting just two of 13 fairways. However, he decided to hit with his driver again and the ball went far left, bouncing off a hospitality tent into the rough. Instead of hitting safely back onto the fairway to at least save a bogey and force a playoff, the big left-hander tried to slice the ball around a tree.

The gamble backfired. The shot hit the tree and moved ahead only 25 yards. Shot number three found a greenside bunker and a terrible lie. His bunker shot flew across the green and into the long grass surrounding the putting surface. A Hail Mary chip attempt for bogey ran past the hole, and Ogilvy had the championship.

After the round ended, Mickelson stated with complete candor, "I still am in shock that I did that. I am such an idiot."

The meltdown at Winged Foot stalled Phil Mickelson's march up the golf rankings, and there is no talk that Tiger's reign as number one is about to end anytime soon.

Self-inflicted Penalties

At the 1968 Masters, Roberto de Vicenzo missed out on a playoff with Bob Goalby after tying for the 72-hole lead. The "Gay Gaucho," as he was called on the tour for his friendly demeanor, had signed a scorecard on which his playing partner Tommy Aaron had written a four instead of birdie three on the 17th hole. The higher score became the official score—Goalby won the tournament by a stroke. The Argentinean's oversight is just one in a long history of famous penalties that resulted in embarrassment or heartbreak and often changed the outcome of the tournament.

In 1941, Ed "Porky" Oliver was tied for the lead in the U.S. Open after four rounds. However, Oliver was disqualified with five other golfers for ignoring a marshal's instructions and starting their round ahead of their designated time. The six had been told to wait, but, concerned about an incoming storm, started the round anyway.

——— ———

In 1987, Craig Stadler suffered the consequences of trying to keep his pants clean. During the third round of the Andy Williams/San Diego Open, Stadler put a towel on the ground to protect his trousers as he played a shot from his knees from a muddy lie near a pine tree. After finishing the tournament in second place, he was told that he'd violated a rule against building a stance. Since he'd failed to include that penalty in his third-round score, he was disqualified. A rules official had missed the violation on the course, but a television viewer reported the infraction.

——— ———

Non-standard equipment can also cause a problem. In 1996, Greg Norman had a first-round lead at the Greater Hartford Open when he noticed that the ball he was using was improperly stamped. For a ball to be usable it must be on the PGA-approved list; when Norman reported the violation, he was disqualified. The same year, Taylor Smith appeared to have first place wrapped up at the Disney World Classic when he was disqualified for using a long putter with an illegal grip.

——— ———

Ian Woosnam made things harder for himself when, at the start of the final round of the 2001 British Open, he had 15 clubs in his golf bag (14 is the maximum). Woosnam was tied for the lead at the time, but the two-stroke penalty cost him a shot at the title. The Royal Lytham & St. Annes course is the only British Open course that opens with a par-three. The extra club was a second driver, a mistake Woosnam or his caddie normally would have noticed on a par-four or par-five hole.

▬ ◄

At the 1997 Players Championship, Davis Love III made a $105,437 mistake when, during the final round, he accidentally nudged his ball during a practice stroke. Instead of replacing the ball and taking a one-stroke penalty, Love putted from the new spot, incurring a two-stroke penalty. When he signed his scorecard, he took only the one stroke and was disqualified for giving himself a lower score than he actually earned.

▬ ◄

At the 2003 Masters, Jeff Maggert was leading on the third hole of the final round when he was hit with a major case of bad luck. Maggert's fairway bunker shot hit the lip of the hazard, rebounding backward to hit him in the chest.

The resulting two-stroke penalty led to a triple-bogey seven, taking him out of the lead for good—he ended up finishing fifth.

Michelle Wie was already famous when she played in her first professional tournament on the women's circuit. However, she made a rookie mistake at the 2005 Samsung World Championship when, during the third round, she took a drop for an unplayable lie. A *Sports Illustrated* reporter named Michael Bamberger believed that Wie had dropped the ball closer to the hole, which is a no-no. Bamberger reported the problem to a rules official the following day. Once Wie had finished her fourth round, it was determined that she had dropped the ball improperly. Because she didn't impose a two-shot penalty on herself, she was disqualified from the tournament. The mistake cost her $53,126 and dampened what should have been an exciting first step into the world of professional golf.

An Unnecessary Gamble

At the 1939 U.S. Open, Sam Snead only needed par on the final hole to win the championship at the Philadelphia Country Club. A bogey would still get him into a playoff. Unfortunately, Snead thought he needed a birdie to qualify for the tie-breaker.

In those days, there were no electronic scoreboards strategically placed around the course, no television crews, no officials with radios—players relied on information from their caddies, other players and even fans to find out their position in the tournament. In his mind, Snead needed to be aggressive on the 18th, a par-five, 558-yard monster, to have a chance of winning the title.

It didn't start well when he hooked his drive into the left rough. He played a wood from the trampled lie and found the bunker 100 yards short of the green. Then Snead tried a full-swing eight iron out of a partially buried lie and drove the ball into the collar of the trap. Next came a smash out of the lip that carried into another bunker before he was finally able to chip onto the green.

As he walked up to the putting surface, Snead was told that all he needed was a bogey to get into a playoff with Byron Nelson, Craig Wood and Denny Shute. Snead missed the bogey putt, ending up with a triple-bogey eight on the hole.

In his autobiography, *Slammin' Sam*, Snead described how devastated he was after he finished the round. "That night I was ready to go out with a gun and pay somebody to shoot me. It weighed on my mind so much that I dropped

10 pounds, lost more hair, and began to choke up even on practice rounds...my doctor said I was headed for a nervous breakdown."

Many people wondered if Snead would ever recover his confidence on the golf course. He did in grand style, finishing his career with over 80 tour victories, including seven majors. But Snead never managed to win the U.S. Open, despite finishing second or tied for second on three occasions. In 1947, he lost in a playoff to Lew Worsham.

Arnold Palmer Gives a Title Away

In his prime, Arnold Palmer was known for his patented charges up the leader board in the final round of major tournaments. At the 1966 U.S. Open, Palmer not only had a seven-shot lead over Billy Casper with just nine holes remaining, but he was also aiming to break Ben Hogan's scoring record of 276 set at the Open in 1948. Casper had already conceded the title in his mind, and he told Palmer that he just wanted to finish second on the Olympic Club course in San Francisco.

On the 10th hole, Palmer bogeyed; Casper settled for par—the lead was down to six shots. On the 13th, a par-three, Palmer went for the flag and found a bunker; Casper played the hole safely—the lead was down to five. On the 15th, Palmer attacked the pin again, bogeying the hole; Casper nailed a 20-foot birdie putt—the advantage had narrowed to three strokes.

Casper wasn't thinking about second place anymore as both players walked to the 16th tee. Palmer found rough with his drive, slashed his way through the rough and ended up with another bogey; Casper birdied the hole—the lead was a single shot.

Another Palmer bogey on 17 combined with another Casper birdie, and the two were tied. On the 18th hole, Casper became the aggressor and hit a long drive down the center of the fairway; a shaken Palmer put his woods away, but his one iron found the rough. Palmer recovered with a nine iron to the back of the green, while Casper's wedge finished 15 feet from the hole. Both two-putted—Palmer had shot 39 on the back nine; Casper had shot 32.

The 18-hole playoff started at 10:30 Monday morning. Once again, Palmer built up a lead on the front nine, this time a modest two-stroke advantage. Three bogeys and a double-bogey on the back nine undid those gains in a hurry, and Casper won by four strokes.

Palmer ended up winning only one U.S. Open title among his seven majors, but giving the title away was only part of the disappointment he felt afterward. "The worst part was that I was very aware of Hogan's record. That was the part that ate at me. I wanted to break the record."

Billy Casper's career is often forgotten. In the era of Palmer, Nicklaus and Player (who were called the Big Three), Casper won three major titles and had 51 PGA Tour victories. Only five players have won more events. Palmer told a sportswriter that he feared Casper more than any other player.

Casper's comeback win over Palmer was especially gratifying for him. For a few hours he emerged out of the shadows to take the spotlight away from golf's most popular player. "As always when Arnold plays, there was a great army following him. But as I started catching him, many of the members of his army deserted ranks, and they became Casper converts. I could really feel the momentum change. People root for underdogs in the U.S., and they all started yelling and screaming and hollering for me. It was a great feeling."

A Two-round Disappointment

Patty Sheehan wanted to win the U.S. Women's Open more than any other golf tournament and had come close on two occasions—a second place finish in 1988 and a 17th place finish in 1989 after being the co-leader heading into the final round.

In 1990 at the Atlanta Athletic Club, Sheehan tore the course apart in the first two rounds, shooting a record 66-68 to reach 10 under par. Poor weather washed Saturday's third round away, forcing the players to contend with 36 holes on Sunday.

Nine holes into the third round, Sheehan still had a commanding nine-stroke lead when she started making mistakes. She finished the 18th hole by hitting a four iron into a lake—the double bogey gave her a 75, the first time in 27 rounds she hadn't shot par or better.

Despite the miscues, caused by either fatigue or nervousness, Sheehan still held a four-stroke lead over Mary Murphy and five strokes over Betsy King, the defending champion. Sheehan had little time to gather herself for the final 18 holes; with just a 35-minute break, she was able to hit only a few practice shots before heading to the first tee.

A bogey on the second hole combined with two early birdies by King knocked Sheehan's lead down to two strokes. The two were co-leaders before Sheehan gave the lead to King when she missed her approach shot on the 17th green by 30 yards. Sheehan needed to birdie the last hole to tie; her attempt fell short, and King kept her title with a four-under-par 284.

Sheehan finished with a 76, and in a tearful post-round interview, she explained her frustration. "It hurts to know that all I had to do was play my game and I would have won," she said. "I know I'm going to win the U.S. Open some day." Sheehan was right; two years later, she won the championship.

Chapter Eight

The Hole-in-One

It is the most ordinary, yet the most special shot in golf. The hole-in-one is a feat many of the most fluid strikers of the ball rarely (and sometimes never) accomplish, while the most average of hackers have been known to bounce them in off trees and golf carts. The hole-in-one is a lucky shot, a random event that makes golf such a crazy game.

The physics involved in hitting a ball that measures 1.69 inches in diameter into a hole that measures 4.25 inches in diameter more than 100 yards away make a hole-in-one seem at the least improbable, but each year about 40,000 aces are recorded on golf courses around North America. The odds for an amateur golfer are about 13,500:1, about half that for a club pro and about 3500:1 for a touring pro.

There are some requirements for an ace to be considered official. It must be witnessed by at least one other person who is willing to sign the scorecard. It must have happened on a course with no more than six par-threes. Touring pros only count the aces they've had in competition. Art Wall Jr. is the king of aces for professionals—he has been credited with 46.

The Golfer's Handbook, *a British magazine, reports that the first hole-in-one was shot by Tom Morris in the first round of the 1868 British Open. The shot was measured at 166 yards, four inches. Aces didn't receive any special attention until 1952 when the American publication* Golf Digest *started sending out report forms to clubhouses. The magazine began publishing the results. It became a popular feature, as average golfers shared their stories about accomplishing the extraordinary.*

Professional Aces

Holes-in-one are all about improbability. In the 54 U.S. Opens leading up to the 1989 championship, there had been only 17 aces. During the second round of the tournament at Oak Hill Country Club in New York, four golfers nailed holes-in-one in less than two hours.

The pin at the 160-yard sixth hole had been placed in a trough, and just about every shot hit behind or to the left of the hole funneled toward it. Doug Weaver, playing in his first Open, made his ace at 8:35 AM. Using a seven iron, Weaver landed his ball 18 feet behind the hole, then watched as it trickled down and in.

Fifty minutes later, Mark Wiebe hit the green eight feet left of the hole. The ball rolled past and then spun back into the hole. Jerry Pate was next, 25 minutes after Wiebe. His seven iron hit the green a foot to the right of the hole and went eight feet beyond before spinning back in. Nick Price was last at 10:00 AM. His shot caught the green slightly to the right of the hole, reversed and plunked into the hole.

According to the National Hole-in-One Association, the odds of four professionals getting aces in one day are 8.7 million to one.

Tiger Woods, perhaps the best golfer in history, has 18 aces (so far), the first when he was six years old. Michelle Wie didn't get her first until she was 12, but has added five more since. Jack Nicklaus has 20 aces, the last when he was 63. Gary Player has 19, his last one in 2006 at the age of 70. Arnold Palmer has 18, his last one when he was 74.

And then there is the great Bobby Jones, who, according to the record books, never had an ace in tournament play, but he had two unofficial holes-in-one. Ben Hogan never had an official ace either and claimed that he rarely aimed at the flag: "I aimed at the spot where I had the best birdie opportunity."

During the 1947 Masters, the great Hogan was paired with a pro named Claude Harmon. During a practice round, Harmon knocked his tee shot into the cup on the 145-yard 12th hole. The crowd cheered wildly, but Hogan remained stoic, knocking his tee shot within eight feet of the hole. When the two golfers reached the hole, the crowd cheered again as Harmon retrieved his ball. Hogan calmly knocked his putt in for a birdie.

At the 13th tee, Hogan finally spoke. "You know back there on the 12th hole?" he said.

"Yes?" said Harmon.

"I've been thinking. I believe that's the first time I ever birdied that hole."

Most golf professionals wouldn't rate the hole-in-one as the toughest shot in golf. The double eagle is much more rare, with only 200 to 250 recorded each year. The skill required to hit a huge drive followed by a huge fairway wood onto the green and into the hole takes the double eagle out of the imagination of most golfers. The ace, however, is attainable by all.

John Daly, who has had three aces and five double eagles over his rocky career, sums up the difference. "I get much more excited about a double eagle, because, man, that's three shots [under par]."

▶ ◀

On the entire PGA Tour in 2005, there were only 33 aces; the LPGA circuit had only 21. That's with the best golfers in the world firing at the pins in over 60 tournaments.

Early in 2007, the hole-in-one was back in golfing news. Odds makers were crunching the numbers as Jacqueline Gagne, a golfer from Rancho Mirage, California, claimed to have had 10 aces between January and May. In 2006, there were only 18 holes-in-one on the entire U.S. Ladies PGA Tour.

Celebrity Aces

Celebrities have certainly had their share of holes-in-one. Bob Hope had six over his long association with the game. Perry Como, Vic Damone, Bing Crosby, Alice Cooper, Groucho Marx and Joe DiMaggio are on the list. Jolting Joe's ace was especially ironic. DiMaggio had donated a TV set as a hole-in-one prize at a 1966 tournament in California, then knocked an eight iron into the cup on the 140-yard 15th for the only ace of the week. No one reported if DiMaggio reclaimed his prize.

▶ ◀

On September 5, 1961, Richard Nixon filled in a *Golf Digest* official hole-in-one form after he aced the second hole at the Bel Air Country Club the day before. He later called it "the greatest thrill in my life—even better than being elected." Dwight Eisenhower and Gerald Ford have also had aces. The most dubious reported claim came from North Korean dictator Kim Jong-il. In October 1994, a spokesperson for the regime said the president had five aces in a round on his way to a 38-under score of 34. Kim is also reported to be able to will a successful rice harvest.

Amazing Aces

Most golfers will never be able to brag about a hole-in-one, or even witness an ace, yet if you were at the Sandhurst Club at Skye near Melbourne, Australia, in August 2004, you might have had the opportunity to watch three in only 10 minutes. The course yielded aces to Ivor Halford, Nicky Eller and Don Curtain—the odds of that happening at such a quick rate are 27 trillion to one.

▬ ◄

Dave Katz became a celebrity for the day at the Pearl Harbor Navy-Marine course in Honolulu. The 72-year-old carded two aces in the same round, hitting nearly identical shots on the 14th and 17th holes. Both times the ball bounced, hit the pin and dropped into the cup.

— —

At Delray Beach, Florida, a resident named Cy Young outdid Katz's feat. Not only did the 70-year-old hit two aces in the same round, but he also accomplished the deed with only one arm. When Young was 10, he'd lost part of his left arm to gangrene. Yet he holed a three iron on the 96-yard first hole and a three wood from 107 yards on the 13th.

— —

In 1995, a 73-year-old golfer named Eric Johnson achieved a lifetime dream by scoring an ace at the Queen's Park Golf Club in Southland, New Zealand. He died a few hours later.

— —

Perhaps one of the most amazing aces ever recorded was by Rose Montgomery. In 1992, the 96-year-old knocked a five wood 100 yards to record her 10th career hole-in-one on the seventh hole at Canyon Country Club in Palm Springs. She shot a 92 that day.

— —

On the other end of the age spectrum is David Huggins from Ipswich, England. The youngster registered his first ace when he was just four years old. At the age of six, he did it again. And two years later, he had a third hole-in-one, this time in a junior competition. Huggins holed his tee shot on the 105-yard seventh hole using a nine iron. Not surprisingly, he is the youngest member of the Ipswich Golf Club.

Longtime golfers will marvel at the rookie luck of Bill Higginbotham of Terre Haute, Indiana. After much persuasion, Higginbotham decided he would give golf a try. The 25-year-old went with a buddy to a nearby municipal nine-hole course. With a borrowed seven iron, Higginbotham knocked his tee shot on the first hole into a hill near the green and watched it bounce a couple of times and roll into the cup. Not only was it the first hole of golf he had ever played, it was also the first time he had ever taken a swing.

Perhaps the worst player to have ever recorded an ace was David Terpoilli of Pennsylvania. At a 1994 corporate outing at the Whitemarsh Country Club, he fired a 123-over 193 that included an ace on the 128-yard 16th. "I haven't picked up a club since," said Terpoilli when asked about the hole-in-one. "How could I ever top that?"

In 1970, the famous blind golfer Charley Boswell aced the 141-yard 14th at Vestavia Country Club in Birmingham. In 1994, 82-year-old Philip Lopiano used a five wood to ace the 136-yard 17th hole at the Glen Brook Country Club in Pennsylvania. Macular degeneration had made Lopiano nearly blind. With the help of his playing partners to help him line up the shot and a bright yellow ball, he was able to nail his third career ace.

Inspired Aces

There are countless tales of husbands and wives acing the same hole and of different family members acing different holes on different courses on the same day. In July 2007, a mother, father and son each made an ace on the same course in Wales within a three-day span. A British bookie pegged the odds of that happening again at 10 million to one.

One of the most inspiring family tales involved the father-son combo of Marty and David Bezbatchenko of Tallmadge, Ohio, whose story was documented by Steve Rushin in *Sports Illustrated*. David had battled neurofibromatosis since age five, and then at age 20, doctors found a brain tumor that required surgery and chemotherapy.

As David battled through his illnesses, he and his father began golfing together.

David set three goals for himself on the golf course: to make a birdie during the summer of 2006, to break 100 the next summer and to get a hole-in-one sometime. The first goal toppled in June when David birdied the 110-yard par-three fifth hole at Congress Lake Club in Hartville, Ohio.

Two months later, David and Marty were standing at the same tee box, playing a round with two friends. Taking an eight iron, David hit a low shot into the wind. The foursome ahead held their fingers inches apart, indicating that David's ball had landed close to the hole. Seconds later they started yelling, "It went in! It went in!"

After everyone had calmed down, Marty hit his own tee shot. The ball flew 20 feet past the pin, spun back toward the cup and dropped in. After much hugging and high-fiving, Marty apologized for making his hole-in-one right after David's. "Dad," David replied, "this makes it better. This is perfect."

That day, David ended up with his first two-digit score, a 98. In a study commissioned by *Golf Digest*, it was found that the odds of two members of the same foursome acing the same hole are 17 million to one.

Then there was the tale from Mark Brockle-hurst in Great Britain who had only one thing on his mind when he began what he hoped would be a leisurely round at the Hoylake Course. He was there to fulfill his departed father's last wish by scattering his ashes on the green of the 11th hole, where he had recorded his only ace.

When Brocklehurst arrived at the 11th tee, he hit an uninspired shot that appeared to fly over the green. "I could see it was flying towards the green, but it went out of sight," said the eight-handicapper. "Apparently it hit a bank and bounced onto the putting surface."

When told by the group ahead that the ball had rolled into the cup, Brocklehurst could only assume that some degree of divine intervention was involved. "I'm not really religious, but I can only think that my father must have been look-ing down on me when I teed off," he said of his first ace. "Golf was very dear to him."

Record Aces

The longest straightaway hole-in-one on record was set by Robert Mitera on October 7, 1965. On an extremely blustery day and with the wind behind him, Mitera nailed a drive on the 447-yard 10th hole at the Miracle Hills Golf Club in

Omaha. The ball was carried by the air stream, bounced near the green and rolled into the hole. The record for a dogleg hole-in-one is even longer. In 1996, Shaun Lynch of Devon, England, aced the 496-yard 17th hole at the Teign Valley Golf Club in Christow, England.

▆— —◤

In April 2007, 102-year-old Elise McLean of Chico, California, became the oldest player to achieve the feat, edging out Harold Stilson from Florida, who knocked in a 108-yard ace when he was 101. The youngest golfer to hit a hole-in-one is believed to be Jack Paine, who was just three years old when he aced a 65-yard hole in Lake Forest, California, in 1991.

▆— —◤

Some golfers defy the odds to make holes-in-one a regular occurrence. At last count, Steve Johnston, an accountant who runs a golf consulting practice, has recorded 47 aces. Johnston has a built-in conversation starter when he meets with golf course owners and operators. "I just have the knack for it," explained the Toronto resident and Canadian record holder. "I've had two holes-in-one in a round. I've had one on a par-four."

An amateur player named Joe Lucius has the record of making 13 aces at one hole, the 15th at the Mohawk Golf Club in Tiffin, Ohio.

The world record holder for aces is an amateur player named Norman Manley. In over 30 years, the now-retired aeronautics worker and movie projectionist recorded 59 aces. "I've always been both lucky and good in sports," explained Manley in a 1996 interview. "Before I knew how to play, I went to take a lesson, and the pro told me, 'You don't need it. You're a natural.' Anything I did in sports I was good at."

In 1964, he unbelievably aced consecutive par-four holes at the Del Valle Country Club in California. Manley's amateur status has resulted in some skepticism about his record. He claims he has never gotten proper credit for his talent.

The King of Aces
Mancil Davis has dubbed himself the "King of Aces," and for good reason—he has 51 official holes-in-one, a PGA record. The former club pro even makes a living off his reputation; he is the Director of Golf Operations for the National Hole-In-One Association. His company is the world's oldest and largest provider of hole-in-one insurance and prize insurance for golf and other

sporting events. Davis is the perfect front man for the organization, and he appears at corporate, charity and other golf-related events all over the world.

He gained fame early in life. In 1966, when he was only 12 years old, he had eight aces. After rising up the golf ladder to play briefly on the PGA Tour, Davis quit to concentrate on making money from his unique talent. He now organizes and attends corporate golf outings, including hole-in-one competitions. He has an additional 10 aces at the par-three, fire-at-the-flag events.

Golfers such as Davis seem to have a knack for aces. "My brain waves are different, much more positive when I'm hitting a six iron on a par-three tee than when I'm hitting a six iron from the fairway," said Davis about the results of psychological testing to discover if he had an innate talent.

Sometimes a little extra luck is required, even for the King of Aces. Davis once hit a three iron off the tee, saw the ball go dead right, hit a small mesquite tree, kick left, hit a sprinkler and roll into the hole.

Davis has an amazing resume of hole-in-one highlights. He has made an ace with every club in his golf bag except his putter, pitching wedge and sand wedge. He has a 379-yard hole-in-one. He had eight in a single year, three in a single week. Between 1967 and 1987, he made at least one hole-in-one per year.

"A hole-in-one for most people is like their kid or grandkids," said Davis in a 2006 *USA Today* article. "If they've had one, they're going to tell you about it. They'll tell you the date, the yardage, the club and how far the ball rolled.

"The average golfer can't truly fathom and basically doesn't have a chance to win the Masters or the Buick Open. But they might have that one swing. They've hit a shot that can never be beaten. It's a unique sport that way."

Chapter Nine

Golf's Worst Affliction

In June 2004, during a European Tour event near Dublin, Ireland, Thomas Bjorn walked off the lush and leafy K Club course in the middle of his round. Asked later about why he withdrew, Bjorn said he was fighting demons in his head and that he didn't want to take another swing. "I just saw trouble everywhere," he said about the course's thick trees and winding river. "The fairway looked tiny. The green seemed to be the size of the hole. There was nothing but fear."

Bjorn was back competing a few days later and put together a solid 2005 season that included a European Tour victory and a top-10 finish at the PGA Championship. By that time he was able to reflect on what had happened in Ireland the year before. "I got out there on a very, very difficult course, and it just got away from me," he said. "I didn't believe in anything. I didn't have a shot that I could go to when I was under pressure."

They've been called "staggers," "whisky fingers" and "jitters," but most commonly, golfers that struggle to make a smooth golf swing or putting stroke, especially close to the hole, are said to suffer from the "yips." And suffer is an apt description. The yips come and then they go, but for many golfers, the affliction is never cured; for some, it means walking away from the sport altogether.

The mental stresses of golf have overwhelmed some of the sport's best players. During a round of golf, players spend less than one percent of the time actually hitting the ball. Walking and waiting take up most of the round. Players have lots of time to let pressure build up. They are often left to stew in their own juices.

Even the best golfers often have to fight to keep self-doubt away from their game. Tiger Woods acknowledged the sport's mental strain. "If you look at reactionary sports, they really don't lose it as fast as someone in this sport. But in our sport, you see quite a few guys get the yips, not only in the golf swing but a ton of guys with putting and chipping."

The Putting Yips

Back in the 1930s, Henry Longhurst was a fine amateur player who won the 1936 German Amateur tournament and came second in the 1938 French Amateur. Then, one tournament he three-putted from three feet on the final hole.

That was it—he walked off the course and never played again.

"It does not come on all short putts," wrote Longhurst in his autobiography, "but you always know in advance when it is coming. I am nothing more than a case for a mental hospital."

The putting malfunction has struck the best of golfers. "Putting affects the nerves more than anything," said Byron Nelson, one of the sport's legends. "I would actually get nauseated over three-footers, and there were tournaments when I couldn't keep a meal down for four days."

Tommy Armour was said to have coined the word *yips* after his experience in the 1931 British Open at Carnoustie. Armour was a solid player, winner of the 1927 U.S. Open and the 1930 PGA Championship. Yet on the 17th hole of the fourth round of the British Open, he missed a two-foot putt. Then, on the 18th, he faced a three-footer to win the tournament.

Armour knew something was wrong. He changed his grip; he held the club as tightly as he could; and he even changed his stance. Armour said he felt blind and unconscious as he took the putter back, but somehow the ball found the hole.

The legendary Harry Vardon, a six-time British Open champion, began missing short putts after contracting tuberculosis in his mid-30s. He tried weird diets, gave up drinking and smoking and even tried a foot-long putter when he was close to the hole. Nothing worked.

His description of the yips captures the feeling of losing control of a simple motor skill. "I would snatch at the ball in a desperate effort to play the shot before the involuntary movement could take effect. Up would go my head and body with a start and off would go the ball, anywhere but on the proper line."

The great Ben Hogan had episodes of the yips that were severe enough that it looked like he couldn't bring the head of the putter back at all. When he finally started the putt, it was with a sudden shudder.

In 1967, Peter Alliss was 36 years old and had already won 20 tournaments. As he stood over an eight-foot putt on the 11th hole at the Masters, he could no longer summon his mind to formulate a putting stroke. "I just froze," remembered Alliss. "I thought, 'Come on, Alliss, pull yourself together.' Then all I did was nudge the ball 20 feet past the hole. Gene Littler asked me if I was okay. I said I wasn't sure."

When Alliss went to hit the next putt, the same thing happened again. He ended up taking an eight or a nine on the hole (he was so confused by that time he was only guessing at his score). By 1969, Alliss left the tour and became a successful broadcaster for British and American television.

Johnny Miller fought the twitches in 1976 while winning the British Open. To neutralize the condition, he put a big red dot on the end of his grip and watched it instead of the club head when he stroked the ball. He even pretended that he was one of his sons and that it wasn't really him that was putting, but his kid. At the 1994 AT&T tournament at Pebble Beach, Miller was faced with a one-foot putt to win. Feeling a twinge on the way, he decided to look at the hole, not the ball. His strategy worked; the ball had just enough steam to fall into the cup.

Bernhard Langer, a two-time Masters champion, is one of the more celebrated sufferers. The German has fought the yips for much of his career, but has still carved out more than 30 tournament wins. They first appeared in the late 1970s, when he was under a lot of pressure to

make money. At that point, Langer was still trying to become consistent in tournament play
with the very real consequence that if he failed,
he would have to return to his old job as a club
pro.

Over his time on the PGA and European tours,
Langer has had three major reoccurrences of the
twitches. "At times my putting was so bad that
people were coming to watch me, but in the
manner of people who go to motor-racing to see
a crash," wrote the soft-spoken German in his
autobiography.

Even his fellow pros winced when asked to
describe Langer's performance on the greens. "I
thought he should have turned in his clubs," said
Nick Price. "He used to have 44 putts a round and
sometimes still make the cut. A good round for
him was 35 putts."

Langer didn't give up. He developed a method
of putting conventionally on putts longer than
15 feet and then switched to a cross-handed style
for anything shorter. It worked for a while, but
inevitably the symptoms reappeared.

For Langer, the yips meant his stroke got
shorter and quicker, and then the ball began
jumping off his blade at odd angles. At the 1989
British Open, he five-putted on the 17th green

and shot an 80. "It follows the classic pattern," he told a Scottish golfing magazine later. "I can putt pretty decently on the practice putting green, but when I'm on the golf course it's completely different. It's like the difference between a practice swing and a regular swing."

The Full-swing Yips

Over a four-year period in the 1930s, Ralph Guldahl dominated golf. He won the U.S. Open in 1937 and 1938, the Masters in 1939 and three consecutive Western Opens from 1936 to 1938, when they had major-championship status. He won 16 times on the PGA circuit and had 20 runner-up finishes.

He was called the father of slow play for his deliberate manner on the golf course. Guldahl was a stoic competitor. As he waited to hole out on the 72nd green to win the U.S. Open title in 1937, he removed a comb from his pocket and carefully rearranged his hair.

The quiet Texan ran into trouble when he began writing an instruction book. The theory was that he overanalyzed his golf swing, and the yips then crept into his game. The formerly consistent straight-hitter never won another tournament. It was a classic case of paralysis by analysis.

Ian Baker-Finch is perhaps the most dramatic example of full-swing yips—involuntary movement(s) when taking a cut at the ball. The Australian won the 1991 British Open, and then his game descended to rock bottom. In 1997, he walked away from the competitive game to become a golf analyst and course designer.

Baker-Finch's problems started when he revamped his swing to add length. Instead of increasing distance, he began spraying his tee shots. Between 1994 and 1997, he missed 32 consecutive 36-hole cuts in PGA events. At the 1996 U.S. Open at Oakland Hills, he shot an 82 and then an 83 in the first two rounds. His 25-over-par score wasn't close to making the cut. On one hole, he duck-hooked his drive no more than 10 feet in the air—it barely traveled 150 yards. On another tee shot, he hit his drive so far out of bounds that there weren't any spotters close enough to find the ball.

Baker-Finch continued to make adjustments to his swing, but a combination of injuries and a complete freezing up in tournament play kept him from finding any success. The final straw came during the first round of the 1997 British Open. The affable Aussie was all over the course and finished with a 92. He said goodbye to competitive golf.

"It starts with either an injury or a flaw in your technique that you continue to work on and get worse," he explained in a 2005 interview. "There were days where I would hit 25 perfect drives on the practice range and then snap hook one on the first tee, and then be all over the course for the rest of the day.

"You're so hurt inside because your mind still thinks like a champion, and you want to hit it the way your mind sees. You just can't do it regularly. You're never too sure when one's going to come out of the bag sideways."

David Duval's freefall from the top of the golfing ladder is even more stunning. In 1999, he replaced Tiger Woods as the world's number one player by winning 11 times in 18 months on the PGA Tour. He signed a $28 million contract with Nike and won his first major, the 2001 British Open. By 2007, Duval made the cut in only four of the seven PGA events he played in. He won $72,000 and was ranked 669th in the world.

Injuries started Duval's rapid decline. In 2000, he sprained a ligament in his back; then came wrist and shoulder ailments. At the time, few people knew that Duval was struggling with his health. He always had an aloof aura—his trademark wraparound sunglasses kept the rest of the world from seeing his emotions.

His physical problems morphed into mental doubts. He changed his swing and began hitting hooks to the left. He sought help from the best swing doctors in the business, but nothing improved. In 2005, he missed the cut at the Bob Hope Chrysler Classic by 41 shots, shooting 30 over par for 72 holes. This was the same event that he won in 1999 by shooting an amazing 59 in the final round.

Duval's once ice-cold demeanor on the course has shifted since the yips intruded into his swing. He seems to genuinely enjoy his rare appearances on the tour. Players and fans alike have hoped he could play his way back into prominence, but his results have been modest at best. There was a glimmer of hope in 2005 when he tied for seventh at the Dunlop Phoenix tournament. But with a troublesome back and a happy family life away from the golf course, many wonder if Duval is motivated to try another comeback.

Curing the Yips

There's no sure cure for the yips. Hypnosis, meditation, yoga and visualization have all been tried, but none has worked on a consistent basis.

For golfers, the yips are an occupational hazard with costly consequences.

Golfers aren't the only ones who get the yips. Surgeons, musicians, dentists, pianists, calligraphers, baseball pitchers and catchers are all candidates for the movement disorder known as focal dystonias. It is simply the abnormal and involuntary contraction of muscles.

In 2004, researchers at the Mayo Clinic began studying the phenomenon by holding a putting tournament for players with certifiable cases of the yips. Jack Thompson, a 52-year-old from Coral Gables, Florida, "won" the tourney with the worst case of yips known to medical science.

It took Thompson 50 putts over 13 holes. He was so dreadful that the other yippers stopped to watch. On one hole, Thompson took eight putts from five feet. "It was embarrassing," said Thompson later. "I was the worst of the worst. I've gone from child prodigy to the most mentally defective golfer in the world."

The yips struck Thompson when he was 25. At that time, he had a two-handicap. He was standing over a delicate nine-foot putt on a course outside Nashville when an inexplicable spasm in his right arm rocketed the ball 30 feet past the hole and off the green. In the following years, he bought over

100 putters and changed his grip dozens of times in the hopes of controlling his stroke.

According to the Mayo Clinic survey of 453 golfers, the average yipper is 45 years old, has a handicap of 4.5 and 30 years of golf experience. The study showed that the yips usually strike good players and that on average, they last about six years. Stress appears to play a major role—the more meaningful the putt, the more likely the yips.

After comparing yippers to non-yippers by monitoring heart rates and muscular readings, a team of specialists in psychology, physical therapy, endocrinology, orthopedics and neurology looked at the results to see if they could develop some intervention methods. They estimated that 33–48 percent of all serious players have experienced the yips. The experts attributed the cause to a combination of focal dystonia and performance anxiety. The study concluded that there was no definitive cure.

After losing the last four holes of a Ryder Cup singles match to Colin Montgomerie in 1991, Mark Calcavecchia broke down. He began to sob and hyperventilate to the point that paramedics were called. Calcavecchia admitted that he had always been hard on himself, even though he has won 13 PGA tournaments and the 1989 British Open.

For some golfers, changing putters and trying new grips will work. Calcavecchia switched to The Claw, a grip that several yippers have found helpful. "Even dating back to the late '80s when I was making everything I looked at, I still missed a lot of short putts because I couldn't stay still over them," explained the 47-year-old who won almost $3 million on the PGA Tour in 2007. "If I try to keep my head dead still, I'll yank it every time. I've just got to look. I can't stand it."

Tom Watson suffered through a decade of the yips and tried putting with his eyes closed. He gradually worked through the problem by forcing himself to accelerate through the putt.

Mac O'Grady, another yips sufferer, donated $30,000 of his golf earnings to the medical department at UCLA to study the problem. "I thought if I touched the ball it would explode like a hand grenade," he told *Golf Digest*. "The nerve endings in my fingertips were misfiring."

The pressure to find a cure comes from the many recreational golfers who have retired and anticipated that golf would provide much of their reason for getting up in the morning. For these players, golf is their main form of staying active. Sadly, the yips take all the fun away, often forcing them to give the sport up.

Hank Haney, a longtime instructor, tackled the yips with the goal of finding a cure. At one time, Haney suffered so much from the affliction that he dumped the game for 10 years.

Haney fought the full-swing yips—he had no idea where he was going to drive the ball. It would take off to the far right or left. The shanks are an even more severe and embarrassing version of the yips—the ball shoots off the clubface at nearly a right angle.

He began studying the yips in the hopes of finding a way to control his own problem. He and his staff looked at over 5000 putting strokes, concluding that 28 percent of all golfers are afflicted. "I'll go so far as to say that on the PGA Tour, anybody using a long putter, a belly putter, a claw or saw grip, any alternative technique, I'll say they suffer from the yips whether or not they say it," Haney concluded. "I taught golf for 25 years before I realized how many people yip putts." Haney also concluded that the yips were even more prevalent in the short game. He found that 40 percent of all golfers had battled the chipping yips.

In 2006, Haney wrote *Fix the Yips Forever*, which documented how he cured his own jitters. Haney believes that anyone can cure their yips by following the drills he and his associates have developed. The book was a hit and led Haney to create a website, fixtheyipsforever.com. The aim is to gather information from golfers from all over the world and perhaps offer some solutions. At the very least, the site is meant to offer some consolation and a forum for sharing ideas.

Haney believes that heredity may have something to do with the malady. If a father yips, it is more likely that his son will, even if they play different sports. The solution includes lots of practice and may involve changing the player's technique.

Haney cured his yips by changing his golf swing. He contends that by making a radical change, he has short-circuited the faulty wiring that led to the yips in the first place. The only way to find a long-term solution is to incorporate a major swing change. "I went from losing all the balls in my bag during a round to playing 150 rounds a year without losing a ball off the tee," says Haney, who is once again a scratch player.

Chapter Ten

Golf Paraphernalia

Every January for the last 55 years, golf pros, buyers and media types have gathered together to talk business. The PGA Merchandise Show brings industry leaders, top manufacturers, PGA professionals and golf organizations to one place with the goal of growing the game.

In 2008, over 45,000 golf industry delegates (the show is not open to the public) made the pilgrimage to the huge Orlando County Convention Center in Florida. Representatives from 75 countries attended the trade show to look over what 1200 exhibitors had for sale. The product presentations filled up over 500,000 square feet of convention floor space that included a huge indoor driving range and an equipment test center.

All of the biggest golf manufacturers—TaylorMade, Callaway, Nike and Adidas—attend, but sometimes the biggest splash is made by one of the 400 new companies that show up in the average year.

At every PGA Merchandise Show, there are items for sale that are on the extreme of silly or extravagant. They often get the most media attention but are completely forgotten by the time the next show rolls around. At least for one year, the hucksters remain successful because they offer a product that just might get rid of the yips or eliminate a slice. What's a few dollars for a device that may cure a longtime golf affliction?

Professional golfers come to the show to look at the newest clubs, but generally shun the gimmicks. Pros call the devices "acts of desperation." And with literally hundreds of new contraptions brought to market each year, golfers must be a desperate group.

Gadgets Galore

The most sought-after gadget, year after year, is one that can help golfers achieve the fundamentally perfect swing. One of the earliest such devices was the Blake Swing-Check that sold for $2 in 1927. About the same time, a company based in Toledo, Ohio, came out with the Denman Rite-Grip. These were basically fingerless grips with a strap running across the palm. They were supposed to correct faulty habits and prevent over-swinging, slicing and hooking.

In 1962, a device called Remind-a-Sleeve was sold through golf magazines. The adjustable plastic sleeve was supposed to keep the left arm straight. It sold for $3.93. In the 1970s, Tommy Bolt, a top PGA player who liked breaking clubs when he was angry, promoted the Tone-O-Matic Hit-Tru Golf Aid, a fingerless, stiff-backed glove that was worn on the left hand.

In the 1980s, a former PGA player named John Schlee decided the right hand needed some attention. He hawked The Secret, claiming that Ben Hogan had unveiled an invaluable golf tip— keep the right hand cupped at impact. Schlee's instrument fit over the back of the right hand and up the forearm. The mechanism was designed to lock the right hand in place to make sure the golfer followed Hogan's advice. It sold for $24.95.

In 1983, an Irish engineer came up with the PuttOScope. It was an odd-looking twin-mirror device that was positioned on the putter head; the golfer was supposed to look in a horizontal mirror to find his own image, which would tell him that he was properly positioned directly over the ball. The second angled mirror was used to fix the golfer's line with the flagstick.

Another putting aid was called the Pro-Gressive Putting Technique, a training putter on a roller. The philosophy was that the putter must be taken back low to the ground, which is accomplished in practice when the golfer uses the roller. By hitting putts in rapid succession, the $258 aid was supposed to foster muscle memory so the player hit the shot properly while on the course.

At the 2008 show, a whole new generation of golfing aids was introduced to retailers. Among them were the Black Classic Bionic Golf Glove—guaranteed to improve a player's grip on the club; At Your Feet—an electronic device attached to the shoe that provides feedback on alignment before the player swings; and the Powerplate—a new-age piece of workout equipment designed especially for the golfer.

Technology to the Rescue

It's amazing what the microchip has done to revolutionize the world of golf gadgets. Better stock up on batteries—golf has gone digital.

Let's start with the Digital Golf Caddy—a gadget that's supposed to take the guesswork out of golfing. For only $29.99, the Golf Caddy provides the golfer with wind direction and detects the crosswind. It can recommend which club to use to compensate for a breeze and even suggests the degree to which you should open or close your stance. It clips to the belt and takes only one nine-volt battery. I haven't seen Tiger Woods use one yet; the pros still seem content to throw blades of grass up in the air and see which direction they travel.

Any device that makes noise on the course is probably not a good idea. The SOUNDadvice is a motion-sensitive instrument that slips over the grip of the club. If the golfer grips the club too hard or swings incorrectly, it beeps. Unforgiving playing partners could have lots of fun at the expense of the poor sod that carries that around on the course.

Another example in the "do-I-really-need-this" category is called the Great Recovery. You first attach small sensors to each golf club and then put the Great Recovery Control Shaft in your golf bag. Turn on the device, and it takes an inventory of your clubs to make sure they're all there. If you forget a club, the Control Shaft sets off an alarm, which hopefully won't annoy your golfing partners.

The SwingHat promises real-time feedback on its user's golf swing, and, with an attached earpiece, the information isn't shared with the rest of the foursome. A motion sensor chip on the specially designed golf cap measures spine angle and transmits an audio signal to help the golfer to stay within the proper range. An adjustable metronome also paces the player's swing tempo.

Here's a sampling of electronic products for less than $100. The Swing Speed Radar ($88) is a device that measures how much speed the golfer is generating as contact is made with the ball. This one might be helpful to the many duffers who are coached to slow their swings down. The Breakmaster ($60) is actually used by lots of professional golfers and their caddies. It is a digital green reader that measures the downhill direction of the green and the precise angle of the slope. The Golf Ball Spinner Sweet Spot Finder Pro ($25) is a gadget with a long name and one function. It will locate the sweet spot on the golf ball, promising the golfer increased distance and accuracy with each shot.

For the serious golfer with the time and money to play lots of layouts, the SkyCaddie is a good gift choice. It's a GPS system for golf that is programmed with 1000 golf courses. The user enters the name of the course and the hole being played, and information about the yardage, hazards and shooting angles instantly appears. The SkyCaddie is one of several personal golf GPS devices on the market that measure such things as the player's driving distance and can be used as a digital scorecard.

Strap Me In

Players can be harnessed, fastened, buckled and handcuffed to an almost infinite array of devices. Start with the Swing Jacket—a kind of straightjacket with cuffs that slide along a rail. It's designed to eliminate bad arm habits.

David Leadbetter, known as one of the sport's top teachers, has built a merchandising empire called Golf Training Systems Inc. One of his gadgets is called The Right Link. It's a plastic device that fits over the upper arm and forearm with a hinge at the elbow that makes a clicking sound. It's supposed to show the player how to position the right arm at the top of the backswing.

Leadbetter also sells The Glove, a white glove with a black strip across the palm to show you where to lay the grip. Any competent golf pro could save you the $25 by using a magic marker.

The Angel looks like two Gladiator wrist protectors that fit over your forearms and keep them together throughout the swing with Velcro. The goal is to promote proper club position and body rotation through the shot. "Flying right elbow" can be cured with what looks like a set of glorified handcuffs.

In search of the pure putting stroke? Try walking around with the P3 Putting System, a long rod that attaches to the putter head and fits around your neck like a shepherd's crook. John Daly's Power Belt winds around the waist, butt and legs, helping golfers "coil and uncoil like a precision spring."

If you have the room for larger devices, you could start with The Slinger. It looks like a robot made of white tubing. You swing under a big circle held up in the air to promote a proper plane. It comes with a head stabilizer, a helmet-like accessory that clamps to your noggin.

Before attaching yourself to any of these devices, you should see a golf pro to make sure you have the right aid for the right problem.

Only the Best

If money is no object, the possibilities are endless. The beginning golfer needing a set of clubs should start with Ping. For about $4000, you get 14 custom fitted clubs made from titanium, graphite and carbon fiber. And those favorite clubs need head covers to keep them warm. For about $40, you can purchase the fuzzy likeness of Arnold Palmer or Tiger Woods to perch atop your driver.

Fashion-conscious women can stand out from the golfing crowd with a $50 glove from Sassy Swings. The hand-beaded accessory features hematite, 14k gold, sterling silver and Swarovski crystals. The beads around the wrist can be used to keep score.

Even the mundane habit of pulling a tee out of your pocket and sticking it in your mouth can be made more enjoyable. Tasty Golf Tees are regular wooden tees, but they come in cherry, grape, strawberry and mint flavors.

To ensure accuracy on the course, you might want to spend an extra few dollars ($60 for a half dozen) on Caesar golf balls. They have no dimples and look like ping-pong balls. A Caesar won't travel as far as a regular golf ball because it's the dimples that give the ball lift; however, the manufacturer guarantees a Caesar ball will go much straighter.

━ ━

For $10 a ball, you might want to invest in Visiball glasses to find any Caesars that do end up out of bounds. The glasses filter out all visible wavelengths of light except the blue end of the spectrum, which gives the white balls a bright blue-white glow in contrast to their surroundings.

━ ━

The tiresome act of bending down to position balls on the driving range matt and rubber tee can be made easier with OXOPOD. A plastic piece attaches to the front of the shoe and has two prongs that are just the right size to pick up a golf ball. After dumping the bucket of balls out on the matt, the player picks up the ball with the device on the end of the shoe. The ball can be set on the tee without having to bend over.

The World's Most Valuable Clubs

How much money are eight golf clubs from the 17th century worth? At least $5 million, says the Royal Troon Golf Club on the west coast of Scotland, the owners of the six long-nosed "play-clubs" and two irons that are on loan from Royal Troon to the British Golf Museum at St. Andrews.

The clubs were discovered bricked up behind a wall during renovation work on a house in the British coastal town of Hull in 1898. A newspaper found with the clubs was dated 1741, but two Scottish collectors believe they could have been crafted a century earlier. The club captain, Adam Wood, gave the clubs to Royal Troon in 1899. He was an original member of Troon, having joined in 1878, and was an avid collector of curios, which may explain why the clubs were given to him originally. They were kept at the golf club until 1991, when they were lent to the British Golf Museum.

The "Adam Wood clubs" are especially valuable because so few of them remain. One of the irons, a "square toe," is one of only two known to exist; the other iron, a "spur toe," is one of only five existing. One collector believes the insignias on the clubs indicate the clubs may have been owned by royalty.

Royal Troon, which has hosted eight British Opens, has discreetly tested the market to see how much they might be worth. The club does not have the security or the storage to properly display the artifacts, but for the time being, the members have not pursued the sale of the world's oldest golf clubs, and they are safe at the museum.

What About Those Tiny Pencils?

Golfers never give them a thought when they grab one from the big container at the pro shop, but the tiny golf pencil is an essential part of the game. Unlike the golf ball, which may have more lives than a cat, the scorecard pencil is usually used for just one round and then thrown away.

The average golf course goes through 28,000 to 43,000 pencils a year, which makes for a highly profitable niche industry that struggles to keep up with demand. Panda Pencil, based in Trenton, Ohio, is the world's largest custom manufacturer of golf pencils. Most of the 288,000 golf pencils that the Panda Plant turns out each day are customized with the club name and logo. Green is favored by 65 percent of Panda's clients. In a good year, they'll turn out 100 million scorecard pencils. Panda Pencil is one of a handful of companies that are part of a $16 million industry.

It costs less than a nickel for a box of 144 of the 3.5-inch, one-ounce pencils. Most of the wood comes from China, the Philippines or Indonesia and is shipped in slats that can be easily milled in North America. The regulation No. 2 pencil is capable of writing an unbroken line for 35 miles straight. In a time when sustainability is a popular buzzword, the poor golf pencil usually survives for one day and is thrown away—not so good for the environment, but great for business.

Chapter Eleven

The Passionate, or Perhaps Crazy, Fans of Golf

There are many golf enthusiasts who take their fervor for the sport to an abnormal intensity. Wendy Keene started playing golf when she was 38. She set up a driving range in her garage and used it every night for the first six months. After playing right-handed for seven years, she became a lefty. It took her four years to break 80, and her handicap now sits at 14.

Committed golf fans are not described by their scores—it's what they'll do to follow their passion that sets them apart from the more casual supporter. Golf was the hiccup that ended Keene's first marriage. "I first proposed that we get a divorce when we were at an LPGA tournament in California," she explained. "He had become a golf widower, and we had nothing in common anymore."

For the next six years, she refused to date non-golfers. It paid off when she found a true match as a life partner. On the day of her second wedding, she finished up a round of golf an hour before the ceremony. Keene has even written a book about the game called The Passionate Power of Golf and Other Secrets to a Better Game the Pros Never Tell You. *Even though Keene was drawn to the sport a little later in life, she said it was inevitable she would become hooked. "I come from a family of golf nuts. I think it's in the genes."*

A little thing like surgery never stops a golf fanatic. In 1995, Dave Derminio, an Arizona resident, was on his way home from the hospital after an appendectomy. While his wife went into a pharmacy to get him some pain medication, he hobbled into a local golf store to hit a few putts.

In 1999, Nobby Owens, a 62-year-old owner of Plaza Travel in Encino, California, decided to combine his passions for golf and travel by customizing a wacky golf trip. The 16-handicapper used the Concorde passenger jet (now out of commercial service) to play 18 holes of golf in London, another round in New York and a third round in a suburb of Los Angeles—all in the same day.

In completing the three-stop, two-continent golf extravaganza, Owens offered some golfing travel tips: "Get a travel bag with wheels. Pack towels around your club heads for protection. Pack your cap, shoes, balls and glove in your carry-on, in case your clubs get lost. As long as you keep receipts for what you have to rent or buy, you can get reimbursed from the airline."

The All-time Nuttiest Golf Fan

Since 1986, the Golf Nut Society has been keeping track of the sport's most crazed fans. Founded by Ron Garland, the society has over 3000 members. Through its website with its online forums and news items, golf's diehard enthusiasts can exchange information and compare their devotion to the game. Several entertainers and sports figures belong to the society. Huey Lewis, Clint Eastwood and Michael Jordan are members, and the late Bob Hope and Jack Lemmon are among the alumni. To become an official golf nut, you have to pay a membership fee and take the online quiz.

Each year, the society names its Golf Nut of the Year—a title earned by accumulating "nut points" for deeds completed in devotion to golf. In 2006, Steve Thorwald, a marketing consultant from La Verne, California, won the award with 71,385 nut points. He received major points for playing golf with his future father-in-law on his wedding day. They changed into tuxedos at the course, going without showers because they were running late. Luckily, his second marriage was to another golf nut—they have matching Certified Golf Nut certificates hanging side by side on the wall of their den.

While recuperating from a hip fracture, Thorwald practiced putting and chipping every day for 25 consecutive days. He also watched every minute of every televised golf tournament over a four-month stretch while he was healing. He has watched the movie *Tin Cup* 16 times with his wife.

Thorwald has made eight holes-in-one over his 50 years playing the game. During the last hole of the match play qualifying round at the Southwest Oregon Amateur, he hit a line drive out of a greenside bunker, breaking one of the windows in the clubhouse bar. After taking a drop behind the green, he chipped in for a bogey and made the Championship flight.

Steve Brown, the 2005 Golf Nut of the Year, won the coveted title with 48,503 nut points. His highlighted craziness included a detour on the way home from a business trip. Brown's wife was ill in the car, but he still made an unplanned stop on the way, playing 18 holes of golf with a buddy in 50-mile-an-hour winds, snow, rain and hail while his wife waited—in the car.

In spring 2004, Brown broke his foot, but he wouldn't let his doctor put it in a cast until winter. When winter arrived, Brown delayed getting the cast again because the weather was unseasonably warm. He continued to play in pain through the following spring and summer and finally had the cast put on his foot a year and a half after the injury.

On the Sunday of the final round of the 2005 Masters, Brown had a long list of chores to finish at his home in Boise, Idaho. He turned on his 10 televisions (living room, family room, kitchen, game room, office, bedroom, garage, shop, patio and bathroom) and hardly missed a stroke.

The devotion of Thorwald and Brown to the game of golf is insanely impressive, but their point totals pale in comparison to the achievements of Bob Fagan. In 2003, the management consultant from Pleasanton, California, racked up an amazing 122,289 nut points. His list of golfing achievements has over 200 items.

Fagan has played over 1641 golf courses in the United States and in doing so, may have played with more people than anyone else alive. He has played 650 of the top-ranked courses in America, including all of the top 100. At the age of 51, he played six different 18-hole courses in the July heat of Palm Springs in a single day.

The two-handicapper achieved the "Golf Nut Slam" by playing on Easter, Mother's Day, Thanksgiving, Christmas, spouse's birthday and wedding anniversary in a single year. Perhaps not surprisingly, Fagan has one ex-wife from a 19-year marriage and about six ex-girlfriends who didn't share his passion for golf.

In 2000 and 2001, he spent more money on caddies, carts and green fees than he realized in total household income. About the same time, he took a six-figure pay decrease to gain an entry-level job with an airline so he could get travel privileges to play more courses. As a result, in 2002, he took 29 different golf trips by airplane.

His weather-related achievements are no less remarkable. He played 18 holes in –35°F (–35°C) temperatures, winning over $800 in bets by breaking par. On a Florida course, Fagan played in wind so strong that it blew all of the sand out of the bunkers. He and his partner suffered wind and sand burns. Fagan once survived playing 18 holes through a violent lightning storm in Park City, Utah. He also played nine holes during hurricane-strength winds—his golf bag kept flying off his shoulder; he had to dodge falling branches; and he had trouble breathing at times because of the intensity of the gusts.

Fagan plays fast. At Shanty Creek's Legend course, he once played through 12 groups in a single 18-hole round. He has played a round of golf in less than 80 strokes on a regulation course in less than 60 minutes while carrying his bag of 14 clubs and walking/running. He played 26 top-ranked courses in Michigan in five-and-a-half-days, during which time he set four course records and drove more than 1300 miles.

Fagan's library consists of almost 3000 golf books, and he subscribes to over 20 golf magazines. He keeps most of his magazines dating back to the 1970s. He has a written record of every 18-hole round that he's ever played and has an alphabetized collection of over 4500 score cards.

His passion for golf started when he was a young boy in a cow pasture in southeastern Pennsylvania. He developed his fairway bunker technique by hitting balls on top of fresh cow pies.

Let's Be Nice Out There

Golf is an easy game to disrupt. Unlike team sports, golf has always provided its competitors respectful stillness and quiet before a shot. No talking, no photos, no cell phone conversations and no movement—it's a time honored code of conduct that has existed since tournaments were first organized. During events, volunteers silently reinforce these messages, holding up "Quiet Please" signs as the golfer prepares to swing.

Like tennis, curling and track and field, golf is a sport with miniscule margins of error. The hush before for each shot allows the athlete to concentrate, recognizing that the act being attempted is so difficult that all competitors deserve a fair chance, whether they are fan favorites or not. It also provides an atmosphere of anticipation that builds drama before each shot.

It is a fragile contract between the fan and player, built on trust and tradition. There have been periodic transgressions of this pact. In the 1960s, Arnold Palmer's devoted fans made life miserable for the upstart Jack Nicklaus. Palmer was at the height of his popularity when a pudgy, blonde-haired kid started beating him. "Arnie's Army" began to take offense. It took several years for galleries to appreciate the greatness of Nicklaus.

Most players try to silently ignore rude spectators. Before a match play event against Tony Jacklin, Gary Player was approached by a fan who said, "You are a real S.O.B., and I hope Tony crushes you today." Player calmly replied, "I am sorry you feel the way you do, and I hope you have a great day."

Greg Norman was more combative toward a heckler while leading the third round of the 1986 U.S. Open at Shinnecock Hills. The Aussie responded to the man's taunts by challenging him to a fight.

Colin Montgomerie has built a combustive relationship with American spectators. Off the course, the Scot is considered one of the nicest men on the tour. He is witty and smart, popular to play with and a good dinner companion. But during a round, his outward demeanor changes to peevishness and ill humor. He becomes a magnet for hecklers.

And in the past, "Monty" has made things worse by responding to the bait. He confronts jibes such as the time honored "Miss it!" by looking for the heckler and calling out with emotion, "Why did you say that?" Unlike Norman, who looks like he's spent a few rounds in a boxing ring, Montgomerie's less than brawny physique offers little intimidation.

Montgomerie was livid with the heckling he received during a first-round loss at the WGC-Accenture Match Play Championship in 2002. He vowed never again to play in the United States. Four weeks later, he was back in America and received a warm response from the fans. "Of course I'm not the only one who deals with this,"

Monty admitted. "I've just got to learn to block it out. I'm able to ignore 99 percent of it, but it's that one percent I have trouble ignoring that's getting me, isn't it?"

The popularity of Tiger Woods has brought golf to the attention of a wider demographic. More people are playing the game, more spectators are watching and more education is required to make sure golf's traditions are upheld. Woods has publicly reminded fans that the sport demands civility. "It [rowdiness] is happening more and more," said Woods. "We're bringing new fans in—usually soccer, American football or basketball fans. They are used to a raucous atmosphere, but golf is not like that."

Woods gets especially perturbed by the distraction of cameras and cell phones going off during play. In 2000, he bogeyed the final hole of the American Express World Championship in Ireland after a camera clicked as he was playing an approach shot. At the 2002 Sony Open in Hawaii, John Cook bogeyed the 17th hole after a phone went off. He lost the tournament by one shot.

The sale of alcohol at events is cited as a contributory factor. Davis Love III had to ask officials to eject a heckler at a tournament in San Diego. "Five times this week people said, 'Do you want a beer?' when I was walking through the ropes.

People assume we're screwing around, but we're not. We're playing hard. I don't come into your office and screw you up. Don't come into mine and screw me up."

Perhaps the worst case of unruly fan behavior occurred at the 1999 Ryder Cup competition in Brookline, Massachusetts. The Ryder Cup, a team competition in which the top players in the United States face off against the best Europeans, brings out the closest feel in atmosphere to a North American professional sporting event. There is inevitably a home-field advantage in the Ryder Cup; nationalism fuels an added intensity from the fans, and the galleries are louder and more raucous.

At times, the hostility toward the European players gained more attention than the golf. Montgomerie faced the worst verbal assault of his career, but this time he re-channeled his fury back into his golf game. The Scot ignored the gallery and played brilliantly. At one point, he told his playing partner Paul Lawrie, "We have the chance to put it back in their faces."

The abuse was bad enough that Montgomerie's father had to leave course, and at one point, Monty's American opponent, Payne Stewart, offered to help control the catcalls by speaking directly to the gallery.

Other European players had to endure fan behavior that was well outside the usual boundaries of golf. A fan shouted at the top of Spanish golfer Jose Maria Olazabal's backswing. Spectators sent rookie Andrew Coltart looking in the wrong direction to hunt for a lost ball. European captain Mark James was especially upset after his wife was spat on during the final day.

Despite all the distractions, the European team kept the competition close and actually led in the early going of the last day. On the 17th green, Justin Leonard birdied a 45-foot putt that put the Americans on the brink of a narrow comeback victory. Before Olazabal was able to take a 25-foot putt that would have kept his team alive, American players, their wives, girlfriends, caddies and spectators surrounded Leonard on the green to celebrate.

Olazabal had to wait several minutes for the green to clear and then missed the putt. It was a major transgression in golfing decorum, and the Europeans were rightly offended. Europe's vice captain, Sam Torrance, called the celebrations "the most disgusting thing I've ever seen." Olazabal said it was "an ugly picture to see." The American team captain, Ben Crenshaw, apologized for the events, but there was widespread criticism in the European press.

The Leader of Arnie's Army

The advent of television made Arnold Palmer golf's first celebrity. He was named one of sport's best players of the 20th century, winning seven major titles and becoming the first pro to win over one million dollars in PGA Tour money.

Palmer's first important win was at the 1958 Masters. He so charmed the Augusta galleries that Johnny Hendrix, an Augusta sportswriter, named Palmer's fans "Arnie's Army." The name stuck. His aggressive, go-for-it-all style made him entertaining to watch. In the new age of television, Palmer took golf to a whole new level of popularity.

Perhaps his greatest talent was in not letting the game stop him from interacting with his admirers. In 1962, he was locked in a tight play-off at the Colonial National Invitational in Fort Worth, Texas. Just off the ninth green, Palmer was faced with a tough chip that he needed to get close to the hole to preserve his one-stroke lead. A huge gallery was following the twosome, and as Palmer prepared to swing, a small boy began talking to his mother.

Distracted, Palmer stepped away from the ball, but once he spied the young boy, he began laughing. The crowd joined in, and Palmer waited until the noise subsided before stepping up to the ball.

The boy began to cry. Palmer started laughing again, and the crowd roared too. On his third attempt, a muffled scream interrupted Palmer's concentration. He turned to see the boy's mother with her hand over her son's mouth. The boy was turning pink. Palmer walked over to the pair, patted the boy and said to his mother, "Hey, don't choke him. This isn't all that important." On the fourth attempt, Palmer hit the chip close to the hole, putted out and won the playoff.

The folklore surrounding Arnold Palmer has grown as the years have passed. He played competitive golf for a long time, which allowed different generations of golf fans to see him play.

Howdy Giles, a dentist from Orlando, Florida, was first hooked on the Palmer legend in 1960 when his then-fiancée bought him a set of Arnold Palmer golf clubs. Giles was one of those nutty golf fans who never strayed far from the sport. He started buying the Palmer line of equipment and then purchased all of his clothes from the Arnold Palmer Collection. He bought his Cadillacs from Arnold Palmer dealerships. He changed his personal stationary to include Palmer's image.

He finally met his hero in 1970. After the short chat, Giles' devotion reached another level. He joined Palmer's Bay Hill Golf Club and moved to a condominium that was located one driveway away from Palmer's. Giles added a deck so he could watch his idol re-grip clubs at his workbench. In 1977, Palmer made Giles his personal dentist. Giles now uses a ball-marker made from a lump of Palmer's gold fillings.

Most other celebrities would probably have labeled Giles a stalker and gone to court to get rid of him. Instead, Palmer reached out to his fan. The two have played more than 100 rounds of golf together. They dine together. Palmer flies him to Augusta each year to watch the Masters. Palmer's wife, Winnie, paid Giles the ultimate compliment when she named him Commander in Chief of Arnie's Army.

Notes on Sources

Callahan, Tom and Dave Kindred. *Around the World in Eighteen Holes*. New York: Doubleday, 1994.

Cayleff, Susan E. *Babe: The Life and Legend of Babe Didrikson Zaharias*. Chicago: University of Illinois Press, 1996.

Concannon, Dale. *Bullets, Bombs and Birdies*. Ann Arbor: Clock Tower Press, 2003.

Daly, John. *My life In and Out of the Rough*. New York: HarperCollins Publishers, 2006.

Jacobsen, Peter with Jack Sheehan. *Embedded Balls*. New York: G.P. Putnam's Sons, 2005.

Kendall, Brian. *Northern Links*. Toronto: Penguin Books, 2001.

Krantz, Les and Tim Knight. *The Best and Worst of Golf: A Definitive Guide*. Chicago: Triumph Books, 2002.

Krugall, Mitchell. *Jordan: The Man, His Words, His Life*. New York: St. Martin's Press, 1994.

Reilly, Rick. *Who's Your Caddy*. New York: Doubleday, 2003.

Rubenstein, Lorne. *Touring Prose*. Toronto: Random House, 1992.

Rubenstein, Lorne and Jeff Neuman. *A Disorderly Compendium of Golf*. Toronto: McClelland and Stewart. 2006.

Sommers, Robert. *Golf Anecdotes*. New York: Oxford University Press, 1995.

Stanton, Tom. *Ty and the Babe*. New York: Thomas Dunne Books, 2007.

Trevino, Lee. *The Snake in the Sandtrap*. New York: Holt, Rinehart and Winston, 1985.

Wade, Don. *And then Jack said to Arnie...* Chicago: Contemporary Books, Inc., 1991.

Wade, Don. *And then Tiger told the Shark...* Chicago: Contemporary Books, Inc., 2000.

Ward, Andrew. *Golf's Strangest Rounds*. London: Robson Books, 1999.

Web Sources

Bad Golfer (n.d.) www.badgolfer.com. Retrieved November 23 to November 25, 2007.

Baseball Hall of Fame (n.d.) www.baseballhalloffame.org. Retrieved December 5 to December 7, 2007.

BC Golf News. May 2004. www.bcgolfnews.com. Retrieved November 21 to November 22, 2007.

Bob Hope (n.d.) www.bobhope.com. Retrieved November 27 to November 28, 2007.

Golf Biographies (n.d.) www.golf.about.com. Retrieved November 21 to November 22, 2007.

Golf Clothes. April 2007. www.metronc.com. Retrieved November 21 to November 22, 2007.

Golf Course Reviews (n.d.) www.worldgolf.com. Retrieved December 5 to December 12, 2007.

Golf Fashion (n.d.) www.scratch-golfer.com. Retrieved November 20 to November 22, 2007.

Golf For Beginners. March 2006. www.worldgolf.com. Retrieved November 27 to November 29, 2007.

Golf For Women. March 2007. www.golfforwomen.com. Retrieved November 21 to November 23, 2007.

Golf Machines (n.d.) www.leaderboard.com. Retrieved December 5 to December 6, 2007.

Golf News (n.d.) www.espn.go.com. Retrieved November 27 to December 12, 2007.

Golf Nut Society (n.d.) www.golfnuts.com. Retrieved December 12 to December 15, 2007.

Golf Quotes (n.d.) www.quotegarden.com. Retrieved December 27 to December 28, 2007.

Golf Training Aids (n.d.) www.dwqualgolf.com. Retrieved December 19 to December 23, 2007.

Hole-in-one News (n.d.) www.hole-in-onenews.com. Retrieved November 30 to December 1, 2007.

Mancil Davis (n.d.) www.mancildavis.com. Retrieved November 30 to December 1, 2007.

PGA News Services, www.pga.com. Retrieved December 3 to December 6, 2007.

United States Golf Association. February 2006. www.usga.org. Retrieved December 10 to December 12, 2007.

United States Open Championship (n.d.) www.usopen.com. Retrieved October 18 to October 20, 2007.

Willie Nelson (n.d.) www.turkpipkin.com. Retrieved November 28 to November 29, 2007.

World's Hardest Golf Courses (n.d.) www.golf-information.info. Retrieved December 5 to December 12, 2007.

World Socialist Web Site. September 1999. www.wsws.org. Retrieved December 12 to December 15, 2007.

Information was also used from the following print outlets:

Advocate, Canadian Pharmaceutical Journal, Chatham Daily News, Edmonton Journal, Edmonton Sun, Financial Post, Globe and Mail, Golf Digest, Golf Magazine, Golf World, Hamilton Spectator, Montreal Gazette, National Post, New York Times, Observer (Sarnia), *Ottawa Citizen, People Magazine, Regina Leader Post, Report on Business Magazine, Sports Illustrated, Star Phoenix* (Saskatoon), *Telegraph, Toronto Star, Time Magazine, USA Today, Vancouver Sun, Vancouver Province, Victoria Times Colonist, Virginian Pilot.*

Stephen Drake

Stephen Drake was born in Vancouver and grew up on a ranch near Merritt, BC. As a teenager he spent many carefree summer days at the Quilchena Golf Course beside beautiful Nicola Lake. For six dollars, he would zip around the nine-hole layout two or three times in a day with his buddies when the course was nearly empty in the afternoon heat. Coyotes were an unofficial hazard; hidden safely in the sagebrush, they would stealthily slip through the fence to grab golf balls as they bounced down the fairway. During years when the salmon run was thick, errant shots landing in Quilchena Creek would disappear under hundreds of spawning fish struggling to move in the trickling flow of water. These days Stephen is a freelance writer and shares space with his wife and two young children.